D1357240

Emma Jane Crampton

Letters to Emma Jane

with notes by *William Donaldson*

and a preface by *Kenneth Tynan*

Eyre Methuen

First published in 1977 by Eyre Methuen Ltd
11 New Fetter Lane
London E.C.4.

Copyright © 1977 Emma Jane Crampton
Preface Copyright © 1977 Kenneth Tynan
Set IBM by 𝓕\ Tek-Art, Croydon, Surrey
Printed by
Butler & Tanner Ltd.,
Frome and London.

ISBN 0 413 380505

Preface

Emma Jane Crampton is the pseudonym of a charming young call-girl whom I met through her protector, the equally charming though far less pseudonymous William Donaldson, Wykehamist, impresario and author. Donaldson had recently written a book called *Both the Ladies and the Gentlemen* about his experiences as a ponce, and I had been good enough to describe it in print as worthy of comparison with the best of Evelyn Waugh. It is typical of Donaldson's nature that he expressed his gratitude by allowing me to entertain him and Miss Crampton to dinner. (An untrustworthy account of this occasion appears on page 52 of the present volume. I shall return to this subject later.) My wife and I found Miss Crampton a lively companion, commendably indiscreet when discussing her professional activities. Now that we have read her rib-tickling manuscript, we realise that there is more to her than just a pretty face and a loose tongue.

Since the above-mentioned dinner party, my relationship with Donaldson has ripened. Together with the well-known director Clifford Williams, I acquired the stage and screen rights to *Both the Ladies and the Gentlemen*, a negotiation somewhat complicated by the fact that, shortly after our agreement was concluded, Donaldson resold the film rights, over dinner at the Savoy Grill, to an Australian producer, from whom he accepted — in what he admits to be a state of fuddled euphoria — a large number of used banknotes, held together with a rubber band. As he explains, he hates to disappoint people. This transaction (known as "the Savoy Sell-Out") precipitated a severe bout of litigation, which consumed a good deal of my own and Mr Williams' time, but in no way diminished our admiration for Donaldson's prose style.

His talent with the typewriter has clearly rubbed off on his protegée. The volume you are about to read consists of correspondence arising out of Donaldson's book — letters, mostly on sexual matters, addressed to Miss Crampton, and accompanied by Miss Crampton's crisp, sassy and outspoken replies. Here, you might say, is a document that makes *The Happy Hooker* sound like the memoirs of a jubilant Rugby footballer. It provides a fascinating inside view of the seamy half-world of the courtesan in the S.W.10 postal district, and makes a challenging contribution to the Great Debate of our time — namely, given the fact that we have sexual organs, to whom should we apply for permission to use them, and how often, and in what positions, and with whom? Among many other provocative ideas, it contains the intriguing proposition that, if prostitutes were compelled to declare their incomes to the tax collector, it would be possible to prosecute Her Majesty's Government for living on immoral earnings.

Returning to the dinner party at which Miss Crampton and her Svengali were my guests, I feel impelled to nail a lie. I did not (as Miss Crampton skittishly reports) address Martin Amis, the younger novelist of that ilk, as "you cocky little shit". I always defer to Martin Amis in everything because he is younger and rougher than I am, and although he is considerably shorter as well, I suspect that he could make mincemeat of me if it came to a donnybrook. There is a French proverb that bears eloquent witness to the warlike qualities of the Amis clan: "Ceux qui sont les ennemis des Amis sont mes amis". Sorry, Martin, and kindly unclench those small but rock-hard fists.

Otherwise, Miss Crampton tells it like it is — a tissue of truths, fleshed out with a brilliant supporting cast that includes Sir Robert Mark, Melvyn Bragg, Norma Levy, Eddie Braben (rhymes with Raeburn), Anna Raeburn (rhymes with Braben), Ludwig Wittgenstein, Clive James (otherwise known as Dame Edna Ebnormal) and Lord Longford's secretary. Like Kingsley Amis endorsing W.H. Smith's dry sherry or Peter Hall promoting Sanderson's baby powder, I am proud to be associated with such a distinguished product. At least it will make you laugh, which is more than can be said for a dry sherry or baby powder.

I shall deduct my fee for this fulsome puff from the royalties, if any, that accrue to William Donaldson from the stage production, if any, of *Both the Ladies and the Gentlemen*. Meanwhile, long life to Emma Jane Crampton and all who play with her.

Kenneth Tynan

Dear Emma Jane,

I'm a fifteen-year-old school-girl and I'm ashamed to say I've never had intercourse, but I do use a vibrator to reach orgasm. I heard recently about a girl who couldn't reach orgasm when she made it with a fellow because she'd used a vibrator too often. I'm afraid the same thing may happen to me when I start sleeping around next October. Do you think I should ease up on the vibrator scene?

> *Worried,*
> *Reading,*
> *Berks*

Dear Worried,

I certainly do. Vibrators can be very dangerous things. My girl friend Big Elaine went to use hers one morning and had a nasty accident. She plugged in the vacuum cleaner by mistake and we haven't seen her or the parrot since.

> Yours,
> Emma Jane

Dear Emma Jane,

What's a nice girl like you doing on the game anyway?

> *Love,*
> *Norma Levy,*
> *London, S.W.3.*

Dear Norma,

I needed the money and it was the only work I could get. Golly, I must have been for literally *thousands* of interviews. At one point I was so desperate I applied for a job as a junior receptionist at

Greg the Hairdresser's King's Road salon and — which was almost as humiliating — as a sales-girl in a live bait shop. A tattooed Scotsman holding a three foot eel told me I didn't have the personality for the job. And that was at Greg the Hairdresser's King's Road salon.

Love,
Emma Jane

Dear Emma Jane,

I'm an enthusiastic collector of erotic magazines and I often read about girls giving their men a "trip round the world". Although I've asked a lot of people in the office, nobody seems to know what the expression means. Can you explain?

Yours hopefully,
Denise Eversleigh,
Hendon, N.W.4.

Dear Denise,

I certainly can, though I'm slightly disturbed, I must admit, that you seem to suggest that this treat might be a gift from a woman to a man. Even in these grim days of alternative abortions, birth control on wheels, supportive sit-ins, voluntary associations, Marxist Lady Bountifuls, liberal interventionists, Women's Lib, friendship as a social service, Agitprop, Grapevine and related horrors, I'm sufficiently old-fashioned to think (saving Kate Millett's presence, of course) that the man ought to pay. Never mind, we'll let that pass. What you have in mind involves you and your young man climbing aboard a suitable ship at Tilbury or Southampton and sailing in it in a clockwise direction until you reach the point at which you started. P & O do a very good inclusive package for two that works out at about £6,975. This may strike you as a lot of money, but I can assure you that it's a complete waste of time. My friend Xaviera Hollander highly recommends it, but what does she know from trips round the world?

> Yours,
> Emma Jane

Darling Emma,

Now look here, L.A. (or the Coast, as we in the entertainment industry call it) is the place to be. I've set up shop in this chic apartment block, and every morning after fresh orange juice and twenty minutes' meditation I stretch myself out by the pool and in no time at all some fun-loving resident has offered me a conducted tour of his wallet. Honestly, I've hardly been on my feet since I arrived! Out here they've never met a lady, you see. You'd do terrific. *So why aren't you here? Everyone else is. Michael Winner, Elton John, Georgie Best, Black Dolores (she wants to be a film star, does Black Dolores) and Julie Christie (so does she). So be professional for once in your life, my girl, start saving and get over here. I'd write more but in case the authorities are intercepting your mail I don't want to put anything too incriminating on a postcard. Letter following.*

> *Tons of love,*
> *Polly*[1]

Darling Polly,

What a relief to get your card! When you said you were joining the Professionals to see the world, I thought you might get posted to West Germany or even Cyprus. I was so *worried*. It's tremendous that you're managing to shoot down plump American pigeons left, right and centre, though I suppose it means you won't be coming back for ages, if at all. This is sad 'cos I miss our chats no end. Dawn Upstairs and Pretty Marie are a laugh, of course, but one is friends *at* them rather than *with* them, if you know what I mean. You are unique in that you *understand*. I'll forgive you for joining the brain drain if you keep writing. Fancy Black Dolores being together enough to shift herself half way across the world! I used to have my work cut out getting her from the bathroom to the bedroom. Doesn't she still topple over every few paces? Give her a big hug from me.

Hey, listen, you know how we used to wonder whether the letters in *Forum* were genuine or concocted in the steaming mind of the Executive Editor? Well, they're genuine! Honestly! From the moment my old man's thoughtful book *Both the Ladies and the Gentlemen* (Calmy Frankenstein, £2.95) came out, I've been absolutely *snowed under*. He's only had five letters, the dear old sausage (four from offended creditors and one from his Aunt Eve, who claims not to have seen him for ten years — I should have been so lucky, right?), but pornographers, liars, oddballs and crackpots have written to me from all over the country. Some are lewd beyond belief, some rather sad, and some seem to confuse me with *The Evening News*'s lively "Pop the Question" column, wanting to know which fucking horse won the Derby in 1923, if old Potato Face of *Hawaii Five-O* is really the son of Helen Hayes and whether Reginald Bosanquet does or doesn't. I shall answer them all most diligently and then offer them in book form as a challenging contribution to the great debate. As it happens, I rather fancy the idea of being squeezed between Linda Lovelace and Dr Robert Chartham on that extraordinary "Sex and Psychology" shelf.

Meanwhile, I press on as usual. In fact, there's no cause for you to cast nasturtiums on my professionalism because by my standards I've been working quite hard. Yesterday, for instance, I made over £100. Nigel of British Intelligence in the afternoon and then dinner with John from the North. Not too heavy. At my age (twenty-four on Nov 14th *hint hint*) I feel a bit of a lemon dressing up as a schoolgirl for British Intelligence, but John from the North is still a doddle as long as you keep off religion and politics.[2] I do realise that £100 won't get me to L.A. but such a move would be out of the question even if I managed to get the fare together. I couldn't possibly leave the old boy in London on his own and the Coast, as you call it, wouldn't be his cup of tea at all. He wouldn't know what to wear, and he'd be utterly lost without cricket on the telly. In fact he's suddenly decided he wants to be a photographer when he grows up and he's been going on at me for ages to get him a camera. He thinks I can't see what his game is, the silly old fool. Men! Know what I mean? Alan Brien came to tea today and went away with one of our pussy cats. Bernard Blue and his little wife Samantha have had kittens. I can't tell you how adorable they are. I was locked away in the bedroom all the time Mr Brien was here. What do you make of that?[3]

Write a proper letter soon.
Masses of love,
Emma Jane

Dear Emma Jane,

We, the Officers and Crew of H.M. Submarine Alliance, have just voted you the woman we would most like to go to ninety feet with. The voting went as follows:

Emma Jane Crampton	*103*
Princess Grace of Monaco	*17*
Mrs Jacqueline Onassis	*12*
Elizabeth Taylor	*4*
Shirley Bassey.	*3*
Fiona Richmond	*2*
Julian Pettifer (remember her?)	*1*
Princess Anne	*0*

Could you send us a photograph of you and Pretty Marie? Pinned up in the mess, it might help to take our minds off the disgusting food we get at sea.

Yours expectantly,

The Officers and Crew of H.M. Submarine Alliance

Dear Boys,

What a buzz to be voted the woman you'd most like to go to ninety feet with! It's particularly gratifying since these competitions don't always go quite according to plan. As you may know, *The Sun* recently offered a prize to the sexiest man on TV called Nicholas Parsons and nobody won. I'm afraid I don't have a photograph of Pretty Marie and myself to send you, but I have great pleasure in enclosing one of my friend Lord Dynevor outside Barcelona Cathedral.

Sorry to hear about the food at sea. When my young man was in the Andrew he got the D.S.O.

for saving the lives of the entire ship's company. He pushed the chef overboard.

>Love,
>Emma Jane

Dear Emma Jane,

My wife and I are avid watchers of television. Being ordinary folk leading sad, humdrum lives, we particularly appreciate programmes that bring celebrities and personalities into our humble living-room. I wonder whether you've ever noticed the extraordinary resemblance between Jimmy Hill and Katie Boyle? I think they must be related, but my wife Dorothy doesn't agree. Could you settle this argument once and for all?

>*Yours sincerely,*
>*D. Tupp (Mr)*
>*Streatham*

Dear Mr Tupp,

Thank you so much for your stupid letter. I must admit I've never noticed the resemblance you mention, so I think your wife Dorothy must be right. I have pleasure in enclosing a photograph of Pretty Marie and myself.

>Yours,
>Emma Jane

Dear Emma Jane,

For how much longer are we going to allow the unions to hold the country to ransom? To change the subject slightly, I'm a perfectly normal married man who is addicted to wearing women's underwear and hosiery. You will imagine my delight, therefore, when I recently got a job in a lingerie shop. I wear pantyhose under my suit and this excites me so much that I have to relieve myself in one of the fitting cubicles several times a day. On one of these trips I surprised a hosiery salesman called Bruce sitting in another cubicle wearing only a garter belt and black nylons. At first he was speechless with shock, but needless to say he felt more at ease when I dropped my trousers to reveal my black, sheer-to-the waist pantyhose. He began to diddle himself, of course, and I did the same while watching him. I have confessed everything to my wife — whom, needless to say, I love very much (photo enclosed) — and not only has she gone home to her mother, but she's now threatening to expose me to my employers. If she did this, I think I might lose my job. How can I get her to see that what I've done is perfectly normal?

> *Yours,*
> *Distraught*
> *(Name and address withheld by request.)*

Dear Mr Frank Swanage of 125 Mellbury Road, S.W.19.,

Good gracious! You're as mad as a meat-axe and I've handed your inexcusable letter straight over to my good friend Det/Sgt "Bunny" Updike of the Morals Squad. You should know that your particular perversion leads to varicose veins, loss of resolve and growing to look like Mrs Thatcher.

> Yours sincerely shocked,
> Emma Jane Crampton

Dear Bunny Rabbit,

Here's another one for you! By the way, you left your surgical stockings and hand-cuffs here last week, so I hope you haven't had to make any dangerous arrests. The hand-cuffs have been useful, but I wish you'd left the key. I had a reporter from *The News of the World* locked to my bedpost for twenty-four hours, and he'd still be there if I hadn't had the enterprise to call in the Fire Brigade[4]. I was quite embarrassed, but they said it happens all the time.

I see that Sir Robert has set up a special Bribery and Corruption Squad at the Yard. What a sensible man he is! So much less time-consuming than having to bung you all individually. No offence meant!

Love,
"Tiddles"

Dear Tiddles,

Thank you for promulgating in my direction the disorderly communication of which you were recently the recipient from a Mr Frank Swanage of 125 Mellbury Road, S.W.19. As it transpires, it couldn't have proceeded into my keeping at a more advantageous circumstance. The purchase of pantyhose I facilitated last week has rendered itself inoperative already and I have therefore effected a fitting with Mr Swanage at his place of employment next Wednesday at 11.00 in the forenoon. I will be responding in your direction next Thursday at the usual time.

Kindest personal regards,
"Bunny Rabbit", Det/Sgt, Morals Squad

Darling Polly,

What a smashing letter and *of course* I won't publish it, or any others you may write, in my forthcoming collection. How can you doubt my discretion after all these years? Whatever is going on out there between you and Captain Kirk is your business, and I'm only happy for you that business is so good. Talking of politics — not that we were — I have to admit that I find myself on all fours (not for the first time, I may say) with Peregrine Worsthorne vis à vis the Chinese; but at least their water torture works. You know how the old boy's been going on at me to get him a camera? Last week I finally gave in to his persistent dripping and bought him one. Disgustingly expensive, but I just managed to squeeze it onto my account at Harrods. Then he said he needed an abrasive black leather jacket and dark room facilities too. I drew the line at that, I can tell you. He can bloody well use Boots like everyone else. "*Boots?*" the fool said, "*Boots?* Great heavens, do you imagine Helmut Newton sends his stuff to Boots?" "He would if Mrs Newton was paying," I said. That shut him up for a while. Today he came home with the first examples of his work (see enclosed). "Who the hell's this?" I said. "She only happens to be *The Sun*'s lovely Page 3 girl Stefanie Marrian as you've never seen her before," he said. That's true enough. As you can see, she's walking down Oxford Street and hanging loose at a bus stop. "Did you pay her?" I asked. "Pay her?" he said. "*Pay* her? No, of course I didn't pay her. I merely introduced myself as Henri Le Branleur the celebrated French photographer with studios in Paris, London and Rome and naturally she agreed to my taking her picture."[5] I'm afraid he's cracking up. In fact we've been on cod fingers and fritters for a week, so I think the old fraud must have paid her a model fee out of his house-keeping allowance. Golly, you have to watch them every minute of the day.

Yesterday I had lunch with Mummy at Searcy's and she said I was looking peaky. I managed to split at 2.30 with the excuse that I had a mass of typing to do for my supposed boss, André Previn.[6] I went home, the phone rang and oh Christ it was her! Do you think she was snooping? I mean, why else would she ring me at home when I'd told her I'd be with Mr Previn? I said I'd had a sudden migraine attack and now she wants me to have my eyes tested. You're so lucky that your Mum's no better than she should be. I'm worn out with this constant feeling of guilt.

Fabulous news, by the way. Georgie Davis has been released at last! I happened to be in the snooker room at the House of Lords when the news came through and I remarked that it only remained to be seen whether Georgie would be gracious enough to grant the State a free pardon. This sensible observation seemed to upset Lord Toppingham (he's still at large, by the way) and he started spluttering to the effect that by letting Georgie out before establishing his guilt or innocence, Roy Jenkins had placed him in a most unenviable position. Absolutely right, I said, and in Georgie's own interests he ought to be locked up again. The assembled Tory heads and corpses mumbled and burped their agreement. "At least the whole unfortunate episode proves that British justice is open to everyone," Toppingham grunted before passing out. "Yes," I said wittily, "like the fucking Ritz."

This lapse apart, we've recently been mixing

with a much better class of person. Clive James came to tea today so it's 2p to speak to us at the moment, I can tell you. He's adapting the old boy's book for the live theatre, if you please, and he'd come to give me and Dawn Upstairs the once-over. We had a hell of a time getting Dawn Upstairs into the starting stalls. "Here," she said, "who is this James Kline person, anyway? I don't want him picking my brains. I'm not stupid, me." When she did finally arrive, absolutely *hours* late, she swept in with such a stomping, show-stopping, high-kicking flourish that Clive said: "Stone the crows, darling, I feel we're meant to line up and sing a chorus of *Hullo Dolly*. Then he whispered to me: "Strike me lucky, this Sheila's really stacked! Still, I suppose a retiring bloke like me would have as much chance with a girl like that as a one-legged Abo in a bum-kicking contest."[7] He's lovely. At one point, he asked Dawn Upstairs what she'd do if one of her customers turned nasty. "I'd scream for Emma Jane," said Dawn Upstairs. "That's odd," said Clive, "what about Willie?" "Oooooh," said Dawn Upstairs, "I suppose he'd scream for Emma Jane too." Bloody right he would, the big girl's blouse.

> Lots of love,
> Emma Jane

Dear Emma Jane,

> *I'm a happily married mother of three, but I recently allowed myself to be taken advantage of by the Unigate milkman. I foolishly gave him the key to my back door and since his appetites are insatiable I never get to finish my housework. Whenever I settle down to do something important, he creeps up*

behind me and I can't cooncemtratx on wxhat I?m
try hell on what I!m tryinx to aaaahg oh Lord it's too
aaaaaAAAHHHHGH

Dear Emma Jane,
Why is it that husbands get up so often in
the middle of the night?
Puzzled (Mrs),
Tooting

Dear Puzzled,

Thank you so much for your letter. A survey was recently carried out by Ms Judy "Adolescents are human beings with valid sexual needs" Hansteen and a team from Grapevine to discover the answer to this question. They found that 26% get up to go to the bathroom, 31% to go to the kitchen and 43% to go home.

Yours,
Emma Jane

Dear Emma Jane,
Now that Angela Rippon is such a success,
don't you think there should be more female news
readers?
Yours,
Mary Hawkins,
Newcastle

Dear Mary,

I certainly do. Reading the news is far too trivial an occupation for a grown man. Leave it to the girls, I say.

Yours,
Emma Jane

Dear Emma Jane,

Forgive my asking, but having read Both the Ladies and the Gentlemen *I can't help worrying about what will happen to your young man when you retire?*

Yours,
Sally Tompkins,
Hull

Dear Sally,

What happens to the hole after the cheese has been eaten? (Brecht.)

Yours,
Emma Jane

Dear Emma Jane,

There was something I meant to ask you on Saturday and in all the excitement I clean forgot. Is it really true that you know Sir Robert Mark's daughter?

Love,
Nigel Dempster,
Fleet Street,
London

Dear Nigel,

Certainly Sir Robert's daughter is a friend of mine, but I see nothing to be ashamed of in that.

Even though her father's only a policeman I've always treated her as an equal. In fact I've never met Sir Robert himself, but I hear he's a bit of a nosey Parker.

Love,

Emma Jane

P.S. Here's a snippet for your amusing column. A friend at the Yard tells me that at Sir Robert and Lady Mark's tasteful home in Esher they have plastic flamingoes on the front lawn and musical toilet rolls.[8]

Dear Emma Jane,

Why are you always having a go at the police? Don't you realise their job is becoming more dangerous every day?

Love,
Nigel

Dear Nigel,

Now they're getting caught it is.

Love,

Emma Jane

Dear Emma Jane,

There you go again! Haven't you got anything *good to say about the police?*

Love,
Nigel

Dear Nigel,

Of course I have. I'm the first to point out, for instance, how, since the Government passed the Race Relations Act, the police have scrupulously suppressed all statistics showing that 99.9% of the company frauds taking place in the City of London are carried out by roving gangs of middle-class, middle-aged whites.

Love,

Emma Jane

P.S. I enclose copies of the photographs taken of you and me on Saturday. You're looking good, I think you'll agree. How do you keep your hair so neat? You've got a head like a racing tadpole.[9]

Dear Emma Jane,

I've always been led to believe that Turkish baths are very good for the skin and circulation, but you seem to prefer sauna baths. Can you tell me why this is?

Your sincerely,
Sharon Pruett,
Crome,
Somerset

Dear Sharon,

Thank you so much for your letter. One reason for my preference is that you can take a sauna bath in the comfort and relative safety of your own home. Visiting a Turkish bath, on the other hand, can be risky, as my dear friend Toby Danvers the Impresario discovered to his cost last week. Feeling a trifle under the weather, he decided to recharge his batteries by planning some Byzantine theatrical swindle while taking his ease in the relaxing atmosphere of the baths behind the Fulham Road. Upon entering this establishment, he groped his way through the steam, took off his clothes, piled them neatly in a corner and joined the orderly queue of gentlemen waiting patiently for the attentions of the Nubian masseur. Then the steam cleared and he discovered he was in a fish and chip shop. "I'll have ten penn'orth of that," said the man next to him, "but go easy on the salt." His case comes up next week.

> Yours,
> Emma Jane

Dear Emma Jane,

You will please excuse that my English is up the creek in parts for I am young Danish girl now living in Holland. They have plenty of erotics in Holland, but writing to big-shot London tart gives me much arousals. Hooray! Most I like the erotics in public, the idea of which appeals greatly to me and my attractive husband. It all started for us one night last winter when we were fortunate enough to find ourselves in a secret sex club near the Hague which we had mistaken for the head office of Royal Dutch airline. Here to our great excitement it turned out to be the go to watch all manner of strange sexual arousals and also to take part if wishing. Quite soon I noticed that nearly all the watchers were men and I felt embarrassed at first, but when the band strike up, randiness set in and I felt better. First we watched a lovely big-shot tart being diddled by two Japanese gentlemen with cameras round their necks and little ding-dongs which they put in her all ways. In the middle of this great act I felt the man next to me, a large Negro in a bowler hat, attempt to get his hand on my erotics. I whispered to my husband that this strange man was putting his hand on my erotics, but he was not upset. He was excited in fact and said: "Let the sooty have his way with you." I would have

*been shocked at any other time, but here I was
aroused as never before. Therefore I parted my lovely
thighs and let his hand engage my erotics. My husband
watched and took out his penis.*

*Soon the strange fingers found my clitoris
and I moaned. Oh fucking hell, what a beautiful
thing! In the room middle the big-shot tart and the
Japanese gentlemen with the little ding-dongs were
flying in all directions: it was difficult to look away,
but when I glanced down the Negro gentleman who
was diddling me also had out his enormous sex. I
took it in one hand and my husband's in the other
and frigged them both. In no time at all I had the
multiplied orgasms. It was the beautiful thing to
come off like that in public you can bet your life!
Since that first time we have had public erotics in
many places. Looking back, I wonder why we didn't
take part in the show; our contribution would have
been welcome no doubt! All I did was frig the Negro
gentleman, then my husband and I went to the car
where we diddled each other; very much better than
usual with the novel arousals we'd just had.*

*My husband and I are coming soon to London
and I am wondering if you could tell us where the
public erotics are to be partaken of in your historical
city?*

> *Hullo!*
> *Lucille Blin*

Kaere Lucille,

Det er netop, fordi did pige har naet toppen
af den hojeste lykke at hun groeder, *Punch*, edited by
William Davis. Har du aldrig hort, og det ma da voere
den skonneste lyd i en mans orer. Every Wednesday

lunchtime. Der er ogsa piger, der af lykke pludselig kan give sig til at le hojt, sa hvis det ogsa skulle ske, ved du altsa grunden. 10 Bouverie St, E.C.4. Say Richard Ingrams sent you! Pas godt pa hinanden I to. Uh! Jeg kan blive helt jaloux!

> Jeres,
> Emma Jane

Dear Emma Jane,

The library here has just acquired a copy of Both the Ladies and the Gentlemen. *I and my colleagues in the Department of Philosophy have been wondering whether it's all true and indeed whether you exist at all.*

> *Yours sincerely,*
> *Anthony Bryson,*
> *University of Warwick*

Dear Dr Bryson,

Thank you so much for your letter. As to whether the book is true, I don't think I can do better than remind you of something Nietzsche once wrote: "What is meant to have the effect of truth must not be true." He was working at the time in the philosophy of acting (a neglected area I think you'll agree), but I see no reason why this observation shouldn't apply to any branch of aesthetics. As X. Trapnel says in *Temporary Kings*: "People assume that because a novel's invented it isn't true. In fact the reverse is the case." Something like that, at any rate. See also Julian Mitchell's interesting paper *Truth and Fiction*, which he contributed to the Royal Institute of Philosophy's 1971-72 series on "Philosophy and the Arts".

As to your ontological question, I can assure you — without going too deeply into the currently fashionable philosophy of possible words — that I do exist in the strong sense *("Es gibt ein ...")* distinguished by Frege (before Russell) from the purely copulative "is" of predication (e.g. "Mrs Thatcher is bald" — a meaningful assertion, certainly, but one which doesn't, of course, bestow existence on old Iron-Drawers). Still, this will be first year stuff to you and your colleagues.

Yours sincerely,
Emma Jane Crampton

Darling Polly,

Thanks for the lovely birthday card and saucy horoscope. How brilliant of you to remember. Not that I believe any of this astrological nonsense. We're very sceptical are we Scorpios. I gave the old boy £10 to buy me a present and he came back with *Wisden Cricketers' Almanack*. "*Wisden Cricketers'* fucking *Almanack*," I said, "what am I meant to do with this?" "Read it," he said. "It's full of fascinating information. For instance, did you know that F.S. Trueman took 307 wickets in test matches for England?" "Good God," I said, "you'd think you could show a little interest in *me* on my birthday." "All right," he said, "how many wickets did you take for England?" In the evening I insisted that we go out, though I rather wish we hadn't. First we wrangled for hours about what film to see. He put up a strong argument for something called *Clinic Xclusive*, but I wasn't having any of that sort of filth on my birthday, I can tell you. He finally settled for *Dog Day After-*

noon, which turned out to be a cracker. Have you seen it? Then he had the front to drag me into some frightful help-yourself place for dinner. "I want to go somewhere *nice,*" I said. "You can't afford it," he said. Oh well, he's a thoughtful old stick, I suppose. The photography's getting no better though. When he manages to get people's heads in, he cocks up the lighting. Today he showed me an entirely blank print. "What the hell's this?" I said. "Black Danielle, S.Z. Corbett and Basil the Black Actor during a total eclipse of the moon," the fool said. What's so galling is that he blames *me* for his lack of progress. He can't do serious, really *abrasive,* investigative work, he says, unless I let him hide in the wardrobe during working hours. I got so fed up with his constant whining that yesterday I said he could be present — though concealed — during a matinée performance for British Intelligence. Just before he was due to show up, Dawn Upstairs popped in to borrow some milk. For a laugh, I let her hide in the wardrobe too. British Intelligence was doing his thing, I was trying to keep a straight face and all the time I could hear the old boy clicking away through the wardrobe's louvre doors (for not entirely successful results see enclosed). Then he sat on his flashbulbs, bellowed like a pic'ed bull and fell out of the wardrobe onto the bed, dragging Dawn Upstairs with him. British Intelligence took it in his stride. "Ah, good to see you 006," he said. "Glad you could drop in." Then he addressed himself to Dawn Upstairs. "And you too 005. Damn clever disguise, if I may say so."[10]

Last week Pretty Marie and I went to the first meeting of PUSSI (Prostitutes for Social and Sexual Integration). A very grand brass with a face done up like a three-week-old trifle harangued us

27

from the platform. She said we ought to be politically more active and she urged us not to work in South Africa or Rhodesia. Who's going to accept a booking in Rhodesia? Replying from the floor, another silly old tart, who'd had her face lifted so many times that every time she smiled she pulled her knickers up, said she didn't believe in politics and had always voted Conservative. This went down rather well. Then someone suggested that PUSSI should publish a monthly news-letter containing a bad-egg list of defaulters — mugs, that is, who'd been known to hand out moody cheques or who were driven by unacceptable deviations. She'd been an actress, she said, and her previous union, Equity, had, through their bad-egg list, many times saved her from working for fly-by-night managements. To show that I, too, had once been of the live theatre, I suggested that in future members should refuse to take their clothes off at auditions or indulge in acts of simulated sexual intercourse unless an accredited PUSSI representative was present and unless the artistic integrity of the scene demanded it. I got the impression that this was taken to be a facetious contribution. Jeremy Sandford was then elected — by seventy-five votes to eighteen — to the title of Honorary Prostitute for his services to the cause. At this point, Pretty Marie and I made an excuse and left. What a lot of nonsense.[11]

Big Elaine went to a fancy dress ball last week as a hula-hula dancer and won first prize as a thatched cottage. Honest. So when are you coming home? As you can see, we're not doing too well without you.

Tons of love,
Emma Jane

Dear Emma Jane,

I'm an ordinary housewife living in the suburbs and my accountant has recently advised me to entertain the occasional gentleman caller in my spare time. Could you: (1) confirm his professional advice that any additional income accruing to me from this side-line would not be subject to tax, and (2) let me know how you are assessed with regard to National Insurance and Graduated Pension?

> *Yours sincerely,*
> *Ethel Pirbrook,*
> *Croydon, Surrey*

Dear Mrs Pirbrook,

Many thanks for your letter. The question of income tax is slightly more complicated than your accountant suggests. There appears to be no good reason why the Inland Revenue should not tax prostitutes on their income, other than that by doing so the state would be open to a prosecution for living on immoral earnings. In the hypothetical case of *Regina v. the State* in the matter of The Morality Act 1876, who'd be in the dock? This question would not present a difficulty to ontological collectivists of either wing, of course, since in their bloated universe the State is an entity over and above a mere aggregate of its members. Whatever such an entity might be — the spirit of the State perhaps? — no doubt Enoch Powell for one, and judging by an astonishing article he recently wrote for *The Times*, Reginald Maudling for another would no doubt stick it in the dock. "I believe that nations have a character and psychology just as much as do individuals," burbled Reggie. "The whole is greater than the sum of the parts, and the national character or temperament does not necessarily coincide with the average, or indeed, with any individual citizen. Yet it is just as real, and it changes with changing influences." Oh dear, oh dear.[12]

As to graduated pensions, I'm not too sure of the answer. I've never bothered with this myself, but my girlfriend Big Elaine, who likes to do everything according to the book, has kept up to date with her contributions most diligently. A year ago, alas, she inadvertently filled up her card with some Green Shield stamps she'd obtained at the local Safeways. She got six months and an electric kettle.

Yours,
Emma Jane

Dear Emma Jane,

Thank you so much for your advice about income tax and insurance contributions. One final question: are you a member of a medical scheme such as BUPA? If not, how do you cope when you're off work? Since you pay no contributions, will they accept you on the National Health?

Yours sincerely,
Ethel Pirbrook

Dear Mrs Pirbrook,

I'm fortunate enough to be one of those people who is very rarely ill. My young man is far from robust, however, and I do have a medical scheme for him. If he's running a slight temperature, I put him on light duties only. If his temperature goes up to over 102, I pop him into bed. If after twenty-four hours his condition is deteriorating so rapidly that the situation looks critical, I call in the old auntie who lives opposite.

> Yours,
> Emma Jane

Dear Emma Jane,
> *What can she do?*
> *Yours,*
> *Ethel Pirbrook*

Dear Mrs Pirbrook,

She can cook my breakfast, that's what she can do.

> Yours,
> Emma Jane

Dear Emma Jane,

> *My wife Ethel and I are an ordinary humdrum couple who watch TV every evening and we have more than once remarked on the truly amazing resemblance between Melvyn Bragg and Sue Lawley. Do you think they could be related?*
> *Yours sincerely,*
> *T. Coombes,*
> *Battersea*

Dear Mr Coombes,

I must admit I've never noticed the resemblance to which you refer, but I've passed your ridiculous letter on to a Mr Tupp of Streatham. He seems to have much the same problem as you. I have pleasure in enclosing a photograph of myself and Black Danielle.

> Yours sincerely,
> Emma Jane Crampton

Dearest Emma,

I think your boss, that nice *Mr Previn, must be working you too hard! You seem to have taken to putting your letters into the wrong envelopes. I've just received one that was obviously meant for a Mr Coombes of Battersea, so I suppose he got mine. Oh well, at least it means that you're thinking of your poor old mother and father! I'm enclosing the letter meant for Mr Coombes, together with the charming snap of you and the other girl relaxing. What a terrific tan she's got! But don't you look* thin *next to her? Are you sure you're eating sensible meals? Anyway, I don't think I know her, do I? Bring her down here one week-end. You know how your father and I like to meet your young friends. Make that charming Mr Previn let you off early one Friday, why don't you?*

> *Lots of love,*
> *Mummy*

Darling Polly,

I think I've solved the servant problem! I've just acquired this perfectly lovely butler-cum-chauffeur-cum-handyman-cum-you name it off Pretty Marie. She was using him as a potted plant to decorate her hall, and when I offered her fifty quid on the table for him she jumped at it. You know how she is. Well, I took him home and after a few days I realised that since I was watering him I might as well feed him too and let him do a little light house-work in return. It was hopeless at first because — under Pretty Marie's deplorable influence, I suppose — he just lay around all day stoned out of his mind and listening to sounds through his silly head-phone things. I enclose some photographs of me admiring him at Pretty Marie's place, and some more taken after I'd got him home. He's rather honky, don't you think? The old boy doesn't seem to have noticed he's here. Well, he doesn't notice anything much these days. He had a medical last week, the dear old thing, and the doctor advised him not to buy any LP's.

Which reminds me: *big* trouble with Henri Le Branleur. Imagine my feelings when Monday's post contained − among the usual invitations to speak at sexological seminars, address the Oxford Union, embark on lecture tours and stand for Parliament − the following letter from the *Sun*'s lovely Page 3 girl Stefanie Marrian:

Dear Miss Crampton, I'm frightfully sorry to have to write to you like this, but I believe you're the only person who can help me. Some weeks ago, a photographer calling himself "Henri Le Branleur" rang my agent and booked me for a three hour session, saying that the pictures were for the French edition of *Vogue*. He took some in Oxford Street (which seemed odd, I must say) and then some rather peculiar ones in a flat which he said he'd borrowed from Helmut Newton, but which I've now discovered is yours. The long and the short of it is that he never paid me, but has now suggested, through my agent, that I send the bill to you. It's rather large, I'm afraid, because he agreed to pay me at the rate of £50 per hour. It's awfully embarrassing having to write to you like this, but I really would like the money. I look forward to hearing from you. Yours sincerely, Stefanie Marrian.

Well! I had Henri properly on the carpet, I can tell you! At first he huffed and puffed and denied the whole thing, but after I applied some sophisticated new sensory deprivation techniques now being taught over here by the Women's Movement, I got the truth and the rest of the photographs out of him. I must say she's one of the most gorgeous ladies I've ever seen, but how about the pictures! You'd have thought that having paid a small fortune to get a *Sun* Page 3 lovely into my flat while I was out earning the money to keep a roof over our heads, he'd at least have had the sense to ask her to take her clothes off. Right? Anyway, I rang up Miss Marrian and invited her over for tea and to pick up her money. I can't tell you how sweet and understanding she was, and — not surprisingly — even lovelier in the flesh than in Henri's silly photographs. After tea I said: "Now look here, Miss Marrian, since I'm paying you at the rate of £50 per hour, would you mind taking your clothes off?" Well, you have to be businesslike in this life, don't you think? And there is such a thing as *droit de branleur*, or so I've always heard. "I'd be only too pleased," she said, the sweet girl. So I summoned Henri and told him to take out his camera and get my money's worth. I enclose copies of the results. She is a buzz, don't you think? Anyway, I've now sentenced Henri to ten days loss of privileges and confiscated his camera for two weeks. I would have been harsher but for an eloquent speech in Henri's defence by Lord Dynevor in which his lordship leaned heavily on the currently modish notion of the male menopause. I don't know, I really don't.[13]

Write soon,

Lots of love,

Emma Jane

P.S. I was about to put the above into an envelope, when Pretty Marie rushed in on her way to a concert at the Festival Hall. "Here," she said, "do you believe in free speech?" "Of course," I said. "Good," she said, "in that case I'll use your phone." The cheeky cat then proceeded to ring a punter in Florida! When she'd finished, I said: "Do you believe in sex and travel, Pretty Marie?" "Ooooh yes," she said. "Well fuck off," I said. Nice one Emma Jane? As it happens, she's becoming quite impossible again, putting herself about and saying she's going to be a film star. That old thing. She met Roman Polanski at a party a few days ago and now she thinks it's only a matter of time. Golly, Dawn Upstairs met Roman Polanski at a party fifteen years ago and she's still waiting. She's bought a Royce Rolls, has Pretty Marie, and now the flash minx drives around in a tee shirt with "I'm Pretty Marie, me" stamped on the front. Next week she's going tabloid.

To: Miss Claire Raynor,
         The Sun,
         30 Bouverie Street, E.C.4.

Dear Claire,

My young man and I have been living together for three years. It's not perfect — what is? — but I've been happy. Until recently, that is. A few weeks ago he threw up his steady job and announced that he was going to become a glamour photographer. Since then he has spent all his savings — and some of mine — photographing girls in the nude (including some *Sun* Page 3 girls, I may say), but he has yet to sell a photograph. I'm not so worried about the money, but I do find I'm becoming jealous. He's still sweet and attentive towards me, but I can't help feeling that he's not *serious* about photography, that it's just an excuse to spend as much time as possible in the proximity of naked girls, many of whom are old enough to be his daughter. I've not discussed this with him because I don't want to appear possessive and silly if I've got nothing to worry about. But I *do* worry. What do you think I ought to do? Show him that I'm jealous? Or sit tight and hope for the best? My girlfriend Dawn Upstairs says I'm being silly, but I think a girl who'll flaunt herself in the nude for a strange man is likely to go further, possibly all the way. And I believe my boyfriend's vulnerable to a younger, more sophisticated person. I'm at my wit's end and I'd really be very grateful for some good advice.

Yours sincerely,
Emma Jane Crampton

Dear Emma,

Well, I'm inclined to agree with your girlfriend Dawn Upstairs and tell you that I don't really think you've got cause to feel anxious or jealous. If your boyfriend can start selling photos soon, he might well make quite a lot of money — (which is probably why he went into the business in the first place). And you'd be surprised to know that some of the models who pose in the nude are very moral ladies indeed who value their reputations and their own boyfriends too much to go beyond a normal professional relationship with a photographer! (They're also in it for the money, and to further a career as a model or actress.)

So even though this is a situation which I

understand could worry you, I think you've got to try and view it as strictly professional. After all, you haven't any evidence that your boyfriend's feelings towards you have changed. Perhaps you could have a frank talk with him about the way you feel — and you might find this very reassuring! You might even decide to go with him on one of his photographic sessions, so that you won't be having any fantasies about what goes on.

> All my very best wishes,
> Yours sincerely,
> Claire Raynor[14]

Dear Emma Jane,

I have a position of responsibility in wholesale fish, but for as long as I can remember I have found it extremely stimulating to expose my manhood to well-mannered women of the utmost respectability. Naturally I have tried to discuss this with my fiancée, but she has always astonished me by saying that it is an uncouth habit, so I have learned to mention it no more. Well, to cut a long story short, I was recently invited to her parents' house in Esher for Sunday lunch and I suddenly had an uncontrollable urge to expose myself to her mother. She was carving the roast lamb at the time, so when she turned round to hand me my plate I surprised her by quickly lowering my trousers, exposing my enormous sex in full view. Needless to say, she let out a shrill scream of terror, dropped the plate of roast lamb and fell over backwards, knocking a bowl of sherry trifle off the sideboard onto the head of the family dalmation — an excitable animal who at once bit my future father-in-law in the left leg. The latter threw me out of the

37

house and told me never to come near his daughter
again. I can't pretend I'm sorry for what I did because
it gave me a tremendous thrill and I've had many first
class orgasms since the incident just thinking about it.
I haven't done anything to hurt anyone (after all, it is
1976), but now my fiancée won't even talk to me.
What can I do to get her back?

> *Yours in distress,*
> *F.F. (Mr),*
> *Wembley*

Dear Mr F.F.,

Don't be too troubled by your future mother-in-law's reactions to your perfectly harmless bit of fun. Up-to-the-minute sexologists now realise that well-mannered women of dignity actually *like* virile young men to expose themselves at unexpected moments; the pity of it is that years of ignorant repression have conditioned them to appear shocked. Happily, the Secretary and Committee of Sunningdale Golf Club are more *au courant* with reality than your future in-laws seem to be, and they have set aside the second week in June as a time when young men of your stripe are encouraged to give the older lady members a thrill. This is what you should do: on any morning between June 8th and 15th, take up your position at the front of the first tee at Sunningdale, wait until a ladies' foursome is about to drive off, then, just as the first lady starts her swing, drop your trousers and shout "Fore!" You will not be disappointed.

> Yours,
> Emma Jane

Dear Emma Jane,

  I thought you might be interested to hear about a recent happening when my husband and I entertained Margaret, the wife of our next-door neighbour, for the evening. Margaret's husband Ronald, who travels in novelties, was working away from home, so we invited her round to our house for company and to spend the night in our spare room, if she wished.

  Well, to cut a long story short, the evening progressed conventionally enough with sherry and small-talk. There was a certain amount of flirtatious chatter between George and Margaret, then he put some sexy music on the record-player (Shirley Bassey at The Talk of the Town, *I think it was) and, having thus set the mood, he pulled down Margaret's panty-hose and sat on her head. Needless to say, I didn't object to this because our relationship with our neighbours has always been free and easy. We are all in our early thirties and have much in common. (Photo enclosed.)*

  For obvious reasons, I didn't want to be left out of the fun, so I pointed out how nice and warm our bed was with its electric blanket compared with the ice-cold sheets on the bed in the spare room. Wouldn't it be much cosier, I suggested, for Margaret to climb in with us? They agreed at once with this suggestion, so we all went upstairs and climbed into bed, with my husband in the middle. Well, one thing led to another and in no time at all I felt his hand descend on my pussy, which, because of the novelty of the situation, no doubt, was unusually responsive. He began to arouse me and my first instinct, I must admit, was to push his hand away. I wasn't going to have an orgasm in front of an audience! George persisted, however, and I quickly lost control — the thought of the three of us lying there naked with my husband calmly diddling me was just too much! My breathing became unnaturally heavy and I launched upon an abandoned climax. I wasn't so abandoned, however, as not to hear similar sounds coming from the other side of the bed! What do you know? Whilst I was having silly reservations about my own husband giving me a hand-job, he was doing the same thing to Margaret! Talk about exciting! Both of us girls realised what was happening and we hit the jack-pot together and in what was for me a terrific orgasm.

George then announced that he would go into the spare room to warm the bed for Margaret. As if what had already taken place wasn't enough, Margaret and I, who had rolled together inadvertantly as George climbed out of bed, proceeded to repeat the exercise! We kissed, fondled and diddled each other furiously. After a while, we climaxed as neither of us had ever climaxed before and yet it goes without saying that neither of us is a lesbian.

Yours sincerely,

Mrs G.C. (Name and address withheld by request.)

Dear Mrs Gloria Chobham of 14 Bradford Road, Leicester,

Yes, you are, and you should be thoroughly ashamed of yourselves. This kind of behaviour is quite unnatural and unless suppressed will spread like wildfire all over the country. In the hope that it may dissuade you from repeating this squalid tumble, I'm enclosing a copy of *The Case Against Pornography* by that fearless King Canute of the anti-filth crusaders, David Holbrook. You could do worse than read it.

His brain dropped out a few years ago, alas, but at least his heart's still in the right place. Take up a hobby and remember the wise words of my good friend Lord Grade of Elstree Studios: "If the Almighty had meant us to be permissive, Moses would have come down from the mountain with the Ten Suggestions yet."[15]

> Yours sincerely,
> Emma Jane Crampton

Dear Emma Jane,

> *Many thanks for your letter and copy of* The Case Against Pornography. *Your advice was so wise and sympathetic that I can't help wondering whether you know Marjorie Proops?*

> *Yours sincerely,*
> *Mrs G.C.* (Name and address withheld by request.)

Dear Mrs Gloria Chobham of 14 Bradford Road, Leicester,

> No, does she really? How sad.
> Yours,
> Emma Jane

❋ ❋ ❋

To: Eddie Braben Esq,
Liverpool, 3.

Dear Eddie,

> Many thanks for the Marjorie Proops joke. I knew it would come in handy eventually and I enclose my cheque for 50p as requested. I'll hang on to "Who's Googie Withers?", if I may, and also

"Nathalie Wood but Mary Quant," but I'm returning the Bill Oddie joke. I can't see myself using this even if the opportunity were to arise, which God forbid.

> Love,
> Emma Jane

Dear Emma Jane,

> *Is Bill Oddie his real name? I think he's an irritating little prat.*
>
> *Love,*
> *Jennie Bissett (aged 6½)*
> *Guildford, Surrey*

Dear Jennie,

> Is Bill Oddie whose real name?
> Love,
> Emma Jane

Dear Emma Jane,

> *I know you're very fond of animals and have several Siamese and Burmese pussy cats. Can you tell me whether the larger cats — lions or cheetahs, say — make reliable and affectionate pets?*
>
> *Yours sincerely,*
> *Josephine Joyce,*
> *Upper Holloway*

Dear Josephine,

> In my experience, the larger cats can never be trusted. My girlfriend Big Elaine kept a leopard for a time, because she thought it might make her seem more mysterious and exotic. (Photo enclosed.) All went well until she entertained her client the Mayor of West Hampstead to a candle-lit dinner. The leopard pee'd in his hat and then bit him in the balls. He had a

42

nervous breakdown and the Mayor of West Hampstead didn't feel too clever either. In fact he didn't call again for a week.[16]

> Yours,
> Emma Jane

Dear Emma Jane,

> *How awful! What happened to the leopard?*
> *Yours,*
> *Josephine Joyce*

Dear Josephine,

> It recovered.
> Love,
> Emma Jane

Dear Emma Jane,

> *I'm a perfectly normal girl in my late teens and I have a steady boy-friend in retail, but I find intercourse painful. I tried using Vaginal Passion Cream as advertised in the latest issue of* Cosmopolitan, *but the first time my boy-friend kissed me good-night it made his lips turn blue. He looked as if he'd been going down on a snowman. Do you happen to know whether there's a lubricant on the market with no embarrassing side effects?*
> *Yours sincerely,*
> *A.F. (Ms)*
> *Birmingham*

Dear Ms A.F.,

> That thoughtful sexologist Anne Hooper of *Forum* highly recommends something called KY jelly, but be careful where you keep it. My girlfriend Big

Elaine confused hers with the Polyfilla tube and all her windows fell out.

Yours,
Emma Jane

Dear Emma Jane,

I'm an attractive brunette of twenty-four and I like to sun-bathe in the nude in the privacy of my back-garden. After a recent session, I went into the bedroom to take a short nap. I didn't bother to put my clothes back on, but lay on the bed, day-dreaming some terrific erotic fantasies before dropping off to sleep. When I woke up, feeling quite sexy I might say, I realised with alarm that there was another person in the room. It was Harry, the young delivery boy from the local grocery store. I was startled at his presence, needless to say, and I immediately covered my glorious nudity with a copy of Country Life, *while I struggled into my pantyhose. His eyes and cheeky grin told me that he'd been in the bedroom for some time before I woke. Well, the bulge in his trousers was quite evident! Just as I was about to scold him for his cheeky ways, the telephone rang. What do you know, it was my husband Christopher! He was away for the week-end on business and now he wanted to continue our telephone conversation of the night before on the endlessly absorbing topic of group sex. For some time he'd been trying to persuade me of the delights of "swinging" but to date I'd always demurred. While he once again went over the good points of swinging, Harry the delivery boy walked across the room to where I was sitting on the edge of the bed, pushed the copy of* Country Life *aside, and,*

*to my astonishment, pulled down my pantyhose.
Needless to say I was utterly shocked, but what
could I do? I was completely helpless. I sat on the
edge of the bed, paralysed, totally naked, listening to
Christopher's arguments in favour of swinging while
Harry started to take his clothes off. I simply couldn't
believe this was happening to me, but worse was to
come! The bedroom door suddenly opened and in
walked Ron the window cleaner with his ladder and
bucket. I'd quite forgotten it was Thursday. Meanwhile, Harry the delivery boy was stroking his well-
endowed erection and proudly displaying it for me to
see. I blushingly stared back at it, truly astonished at
its magnificent proportions. Ron the window cleaner
then took down his trousers and brazenly placed my
hand on his throbbing member. Just then, my husband
Christopher asked me if everything was all right. What
could I say? He would never believe that this could be
happening to me of all people! My hand froze and I
meekly answered that everything was just fine. Meanwhile, Harry the delivery boy was stroking my lovely
thighs, while Roger the TV repair man fondled my
glorious breasts. As I continued to listen to my
husband's increasingly insistent arguments in favour
of swinging, Greg the telephone engineer pushed me
roughly back on the bed. Needless to say, I struggled
furiously as he began to diddle my exquisite* mons
Venus, *fearful that my husband would suspect that I
was up to something. It was no good. I couldn't
suppress my own perfectly natural desires. "No!
no!" I cried, but it was too late. I dropped the phone,
and, sobbing and groaning in ecstasy, I climaxed like
I've never climaxed before. When my husband came
home after the week-end, I told him all about my
experience and do you know what? He was convinced*

that I'd made the whole thing up just to please him and he's still trying to persuade me to swing!

> *Yours,*
> *B.B. (Mrs)*
> *Croydon,*
> *Surrey*

To: Phillip Hodson Esq,
        Forum,
        2 Bramber Road, W.14.

Dear Phillip,

       For the last time, I must ask you to stop sending me your absurd letters. I know it winds you up to write them, but it really pisses me off having to read the silly things. I'm trying to run a business here, so cut it out, there's a good boy.[17]

> Love,
> Emma Jane

Dear Emma Jane,

       Do you watch That's Life *with Esther Rantzen? In my opinion it's a pornographic programme. Last week there were twenty-three sniggering references to "knickers" and seventy-five roguish allusions to "tits".*

> *Disgusted,*
> *The Climax Bookshop,*
> *Charing Cross Road,*
> *London, W.1.*

Dear Disgusted,

      Seventy-six, but who's counting?

      Love,

      Emma Jane

❋   ❋   ❋

To: Miss Esther Rantzen,
        The BBC,
        Kensington House, W.14.

Dear Miss Rantzen,

      In my opinion *That's Life* is a pornographic programme. Last week there were twenty-three sniggering references to knickers and seventy-six roguish allusions to tits.

      Yours sincerely,

      Emma Jane Crampton

Dear Emma Jane,

      Thank you very much for your letter. Your comments were so helpful and encouraging — I am most grateful to you for having taken the trouble to write to me.

      May I in return send you my best wishes.

      Yours sincerely,

      Esther Rantzen [18]

Dear Emma Jane,

      Thank you so much for the advice about the KY jelly. Alas, my problem persisted, so I went to the Post Office to fill in the relevant application forms. After some delay, they gave me permission to see a doctor, and this I did. He examined me from top to toe but when he had finished he seemed as perplexed as when I arrived. "I'm terribly sorry," he said, "but

*I'm quite unable to diagnose the trouble. I think it
must be too much to drink." What should I do now?*

> *Yours,*
> *A.F. (Ms),*
> *Bath,*
> *Somerset*

Dear Ms A.F.,

> Go back when he's sober.
> Yours,
> Emma Jane

Dear Emma Jane,

*I've got a problem which no one seems
able to solve. I've written to many eminent sexologists, including Ms Anna Raeburn, Miss Fiona
Richmond, Ms Irma Kurtz, The Reverend Chad Varah
and Mr Malcolm Allison, but none of them seems able
to help. You're my last hope. The fact is I'm married
to one of those immature women who is quite unable
to settle down in a one-to-one relationship as advertised
by the Government. After seven years of marriage she
still likes nudity and violence, pornographic books
and films, Michael Parkinson, pot parties, strange men
and plenty of sexual variety — but only outside the
home. What makes me really uptight about the
situation is that I like the same things (except men,
needless to say), but when I point this out to her she
gets angry. In fact, as far as she's concerned I'm
supposed to behave like an old-fashioned married
man. When I explain that since the Sexual Relations
Act 1976 became law times have changed, she says
not in her home they haven't. What makes it worse is
that in the last seven years her attitude to sex has
become utterly selfish. She only screws me when she*

*wants it, never when I do, and she doesn't bother
with any of the loving preliminaries as specified in the
manuals, not even a kiss. It's crash bang wallop and
all over in a second. When I read about the mutual
satisfaction now being enjoyed by such ideal couples
as Mr Cliff Richard, Starsky and Hutch, Mr and Mrs
Larry Lamb and Prince Rainier and Gene Kelly, I get
thoroughly frustrated. Before we were married, she
was very passionate and loving, but she cut all that
out after our honeymoon. When I tell her that for
me our sex life is utterly unsatisfactory, she says
that that's the way it is when people are married.
I may be naive, but I'm not that naive, especially
when I know she's having a ball when she's away
from home on business. I'm as sexually liberated
as any woman, but what use is it if I have a wife
who doesn't want me?*
> *Depressed*
> *Portsmouth*

Dear Depressed,

     I assume you're an attractive man with a
healthy instinct for sex, so it seems to me that you
have only two alternatives: either change your wife's
attitude towards you or dump her and find yourself a
new lover. I can't help feeling, though, that some of
the fault may be yours. You say you are as sexually
liberated as any woman, but just how resourceful are
you at putting this liberation into practice? Most men
believe that when it comes to sex women are machines
who can enjoy it at any time and in any sort of
situation, but this is by no means always the case,
you know. After a hard day at the office, a woman
has to be eased tactfully into a responsive mood.
Bearing this in mind, take a little trouble over how

you set the scene: arrange some helpful props now and then, such as a romantic dinner *à deux*, or prepare a warm bubble-bath for her and then offer to give her a topless V.I.P. massage. Or, when she arrives home from work one night, have some sexy music already on the record-player and greet her at the front-door dressed only in your most audacious underwear. I know that this advice is not exactly new, but it's important that you remind her that you're every bit as much of a sex object as the saucy boys at the office or the male models who flaunt themselves in those pornographic films you mention. But remember this: sex isn't just something she does to you. It's what you do *together*. Take the lead sometimes. Thoughtful husbands spend a lot of time thinking up new ways of being exciting. Be provocative! Walk around naked while doing the housework. When you meet her at a smart restaurant or bar give her the surprise of her life when you take your overcoat off! Driving home in the car, slip your hand up the back of her blouse and snap her bra elastic! If she does the same to you, laugh encouragingly and ask her to do it again. But don't rely entirely on your physical attributes. Never play the dumb cowboy if you are brainy. You'll be conning her and conning yourself and that's no basis for a good relationship. If she wants a cowboy you'd be better off without each other. Stand up for your beliefs. If she says they should bring back rape, there's no such thing as capital punishment and that it takes two to commit Mrs Whitehouse, let her know you disagree. She'll respect you for it in the long run. There are certain things, however, that no bright man ever says to the woman in his life. These are:

I've got a headache.

You've got a headache.

The parrot's got a headache.

No, not like that, like *this*.

You've just broken the world speed record.

You're going bald on top.

You said you'd be home an hour ago.

Flats don't clean themselves, you know.

You never say you love me any more.

Did you see the huge diamond Julia gave John?

Women need constant variety, so you could try having an AC/DC, TV, DIY, ITV, BBC, CP, S/M, CI threesome with the lad from the bakery, but *only* if the idea turns you on as well. Always remember that, as in cooking, everything is all right in sex *just so long as* all parties are enjoying themselves. (Read my forthcoming book *A Hundred Ways to Goose a Cook*, which is to be published shortly with a notably illiterate introduction by Shirley Conran and photographs by Henri Le Branleur.[19] If your wife won't change her ways, start going out yourself whenever she does, and when you come home don't give her any explanation as to where you've been. Then she might stop regarding you as just part of the household furniture.

Good luck,
Emma Jane

Darling Polly,

Oh my, it was Dr Leavis's eightieth birthday last Thursday and the old boy went quite off his rocker. Made me cancel all my bookings, which delighted me, of course, until he explained the day's programme. Long bicycle ride in the morning. Then lunch, consisting of home-baked biscuits and parsnip wine. (Golly, a spoonful of that would pump out Loch Ness, I can tell you.) In the afternoon the fool read to me from *English Literature in Our Time and the University*.[20] Ian Robinson came to tea. Rather a serious man, I thought. Then back on our fucking bicycles and round to Fitzroy Square where we ritually burned a dozen copies of *The Common Reader* and *Eminent Victorians*. "What are we doing here?" I asked. "Making our small protest against personal relationships, elitism and sexual tolerance," he said. Back home in time to hear the tribute on BBC radio and then he made me write out a hundred times: "I will not commit the intentional fallacy." In bed by 10 p.m. and good Knights. I think I'd rather have worked, and that's something I never thought I'd say.

It's all go at the moment 'cos on Monday night we dined with Ken Tynan and his lovely wife Kathleen: an elegant occasion, with the old boy and I lowering the tone, I thought, by only the merest fraction. I suppose one shouldn't mention a lady's looks in these days of Women's Lib, but Mrs Tynan's *devastating*. Apart from us, much the usual crowd. Mr and Mrs John Mortimer, Penelope Gilliatt, Angela Huth and Kingsley's boy, Martin. John Mortimer was most cordial towards me, which was very sporting of him considering I hadn't seen him since I appeared — to no avail, alas — as an expert witness for the prosecution at the Linda Lovelace trial. Did I tell you about that? Anyway, over dinner Tynan asserted that the cinema had not so far produced an original work of art about the human condition. The only great films, he argued, had been thrillers, westerns, comedies or musicals. "You mean *genre* films," said Martin

Amis. "I know what I mean, you cocky little shit," said Tynan, "and take your elbows off the table or you won't get any pudding." Mrs Gilliatt seemed disposed to argue the matter, but she was unable to come up with an example refuting Tynan's theory. John Mortimer was then very cogent on the subject of Sir Robert Mark's bizarre handling of statistics. He pointed out that when delivering his astonishing "too many acquittals" speech, Sir Robert had completely ignored the time honoured prosecution tactic of over-icing the cake by smothering the defendant under an avalanche of alternative charges, in order to impress the jury with the gravity of the situation. Although these extra charges are often dismissed, they stay on the record and add substantially to Sir Robert's not-guilty figures. What a foolish man he is.

Alas, I was compelled to leave this stimulating dinner party rather early since I had previously agreed to take part in a *tableau vivant* with Dawn Upstairs for two young men in self-adhesive tiles. Dawn Upstairs was going through the motions, I was moaning in simulated ecstasy and the mugs seemed well pleased, when Dawn Upstairs suddenly popped her head up between my legs and said: "It's the Queen Mother I feel sorry for." I think her mind must have been more on Lord and Lady Snowdon's present difficulties than on the job in hand. Well, I got the giggles, of course, and one of the punters, who'd just taken his trousers off, thought I was laughing at him. He got the hump and they threw us out without recompense. I'm taking the matter up with PUSSI.[21]

> Write soon,
> Lots of love,
> Emma Jane

Dear Emma Jane,

Hi there lovely! I've just finished reading your old man's magnus opus The Gents and Ladies and all I can say is "Wow!" and "Hot damn!" If there were more girls around like you, sweetheart, there'd be a lot fewer characters having to change their pyjama bottoms in the morning, you follow me honey?

Now it seems to me from reading the afore-mentioned magnus opus that a lot of cats have been into your pants, but most of them didn't exactly play your pipes the way you'd like them played! There was no mention, at least, of guys who really made your bells ring! Right? Well, how would you react to a small wager? I'll pick up the bill for one hell of an evening on the town, including a steak dinner and choice of wines, on condition that you *pay* me *if I turn out to have the biggest dong and best loving technique you ever experienced, sweetheart! I know this sounds kind of big-headed of me, but you're going to find out that I've got the biggest cock in the country and when I put it in you, well baby, you're really going to see stars!*

Just one thing. Please be sure to reply to me care of my *business address. My lady wife Mary (née Morgan) knows I've read your pooped-out protector's book and she's sure to figure out what her horny-handed old husband's up to!* [22]

Yours for mutual pleasure,
Richard Ingrams,
London, W.1.

To: Richard Ingrams Esq,
        Private Eye,
        34 Greek Street,
        London, W.1.

Dear Mr Ingrams,

Miss Emma Jane Crampton is on a lecture tour of the United States at the moment, but she has asked me to reply to your kind letter of August 4th. She thanks you for your contribution but wishes me to point out that it's not exactly the sort of material she is looking for at the moment. She does feel you should be encouraged, however, and she suggests you send further examples of your work to Futura Publications Ltd, [23] 110 Warner Road, London S.E.5. They are currently planning a refreshingly frank new series of dong-tickling books under the general title "The Confessions of a Randy Condom Salesman" and Miss Crampton thinks that you might well have a mutually beneficial business relationship.

Yours sincerely,
Lady Jackie Wolverhampton-Jones
(Secretary to Miss Emma Jane Crampton)

Dear Emma Jane,

Sentencing three men at Bodmin Crown Court, Mr Justice Ackner told them that a factor behind their appalling behaviour was the "stimulus of dirty books which all of you read." He added: "For those who think that pornography can have no effect on crime, this is an indication of how wrong they can be."

What, I wonder, do the filth merchants have to say about that?

Yours sincerely,
Philip Wrack, [23]
"The Column with the Sunday Punch",
The News of the World,
London, E.C.4.

Dear Mr Wrack,

Speaking for myself, I'd say you might be suffering from a slight lesion of the brain. A second opinion never hurts, however, so I have forwarded your letter to my good friend Ivor Mills, Professor of Medicine at Cambridge University.[25] In a forceful letter to *The Times*, Professor Mills recently said that he knew of "*no* data supporting the view that erotic material is harmful to the young . . . If Dr Ellison, or the Responsible Society for whom he speaks, know of such facts they should present them to us . . . The American studies of people convicted of sexual crimes indicated that they had been *deprived* of sexual education when young." Still, what would a woolly-minded egghead, shut away in his academic ivory tower, know about *real* people and *real* problems? With this in mind, I have also written on your behalf to Miss Marjorie Proops. Unlike Professor Mills, she's a wise old tart who's helped more people with her homely advice than all your fancy psychiatrists with their long words and funny names.

Yours sincerely,

Emma Jane Crampton

P.S. Having occasion recently to sentence my young man to four days loss of privileges, I told him that a factor behind his appalling behaviour (he'd stayed out after sunset without a signed pass) was the stimulus of an amusing Moselle he'd taken at White's while lunching there with his friend Lord Dynevor. What, I wonder, do the wine merchants have to say about that?

❋ ❋ ❋

To: Miss Marjorie Proops,
Daily Mirror,
London, E.C.1.

Dear Miss Proops,

Sentencing three men at Bodmin Crown Court, Mr Justice Ackner told them that a factor behind their appalling behaviour was "The stimulus of dirty books which all of you read." He added: "For those who think that pornography can have no effect on crime, this is an indication of how wrong they can be."

What, I wonder, do the filth merchants have to say about that?

Yours sincerely,
Emma Jane Crampton

Dear Miss Crampton,

Thank you for your letter. Judges are, of course, entitled to their opinions, but no one is obliged to agree with the comments they make on questions of this sort. While I would not deny their ability or right to interpret the law, I would question their comments on matters they are not especially qualified to talk about.

It would be impossible for me to draw any conclusion from this case as I do not know what exactly was meant by pornography. Many people consider books that are mildly titillating as pornographic. Equally, there are publications available which could well be harmful if read by a small minority of people.

With kind regards,
Yours sincerely,
Marjorie Proops [26]

Dear Emma Jane,

I am a lovely young woman of twenty-two who would very much like to become a call-girl. I reckon I have all the right physical attributes, but I was never certain I wanted to be a prostitute until I read Both the Ladies and the Gentlemen. *Now my mind is made up. The way of life sounds really exhilarating, with lots of laughs and a few perversions, but that's natural, I suppose.*

Can you advise me on how to get started?
Yours,
Marigold Hughes-Rhys,
The Old Coach House,
Swindon,
Wilts.

Dear Marigold,

I'm truly appalled that reading such a shallow, ill-researched book should have made you think I would *ever* be so irresponsible as to advise a girl to take up the way of life. Embarked on carelessly, it can lead only to the most terrible and tragic consequences. Let me tell you about my close friend Dopey Linda. After just six months on the game she was unrecognisable as the pretty, laughing, carefree young woman who one night, as the result of a silly bet, accepted £25 to go to bed with a gentleman from the Russian Embassy. Her looks had gone, she'd become a shambling, bleary-eyed misfit, bumping into the furniture and given to bouts of hysterical laughter alternating with moods of black depression. Now she's no more than a vegetable, rambling on incoherently, unable to tell right from wrong, good from bad or Dickins from Jones. She's a walking tragedy,

serving no purpose other than to act as a grim warning
to thoughtless young girls like yourself.

> Yours sincerely,
> Emma Jane Crampton

Dear Emma Jane,

> *How terrible! Your letter has made me feel
so silly. Where is the poor girl now? I'd like to visit
her to see if I could help.*

>> *Yours,*
>> *Marigold Hughes-Rhys*

Dear Marigold,

> She's Creative Director of London's third
largest advertising agency and in her spare time writes
speeches for Lord Hailsham. [27]

>> Yours,
>> Emma Jane

Dear Emma Jane,

> *How old's your young man?*
>> *Yours,*
>> *Sabrina Worth,*
>> *Poole, Dorset*

Dear Sabrina,

> He's the same age as Donald Duck. England's
Test Selectors please note.

>> Love,
>> Emma Jane

Dear Emma Jane,

Our eldest, Jackie, is twelve and we are beginning to wonder about schools. Could you give us any useful advice on the subject?

Yours hopefully,
Noreen Kray,
Station Road,
Hoxton

Dear Mrs Kray,

About Jackie's education: it must be Eton, Harrow or Winchester, of course, though not necessarily in that order. It's often best to start with Winchester and then go on to Eton or Harrow when you get thrown out of Winchester for failing to come up to the required academic standard. I have some experience of all three schools, as it happens, in that my young man went to Winchester, his nephew Gerard went to Harrow and my young step-son Charlie is presently at Eton. The trouble is that none of them seems to have turned out too well. My young man's a ponce, his nephew Gerard is about to join the Metropolitan Police (strange; I wouldn't have thought of him as a businessman), and my young step-son Charlie sleeps in his jewellery and wants to be a rock 'n roll singer.[28]

To help you in your difficult choice I don't think I can do better than pass on a story that was all the go in my dear Mother's day. Many years ago, it was the rather jolly custom for Eton, Harrow and Winchester to play one another at cricket during the same week at Lords. It was a feature of the London season, don't you know? Anyway, one afternoon an Etonian, a Harrovian and a Wykehamist were peacefully watching the cricket from the pavilion, when a young lady entered who had nowhere to sit. The

Etonian at once offered her a chair, the Wykehamist
dutifully fetched it and the Harrovian sat on it.

Yours sincerely,

Emma Jane Crampton

Dear Emma Jane,

Thank you so much for your helpful letter.
Perhaps I should have explained, however, that
Jackie is a girl.

Yours sincerely,

Noreen Kray

Dear Mrs Kray,

Golly, if I'd known that, I would naturally
have recommended Stowe. (Photo enclosed.)

Yours,

Emma Jane

Dear Emma Jane,

My husband is just as sweet and attentive as
ever, but he doesn't seem to desire me physically any
more. Is there anything I can do?

Frustrated,

Ryde,

Isle of Wight

Dear Frustrated,

Not a lot. Wasn't it Marjorie Proops who
wrote of "all the sullen ardour of a husband obliging
himself to make love to his wife in the thick of carnal
indifference"? [29] Be that as it may, I suppose you
could try out one of the floor routines recommended
in that nonsensical book *The Joy of Sex*. This should

give you both a laugh, and laughter— for reasons I've never clearly understood — is meant to be an aphrodisiac. If you turn to page 139, for instance, you'll find a position that ought to have you in stitches — literally. (Igor Frolik tried it in training, and look what happened to her in Montreal.) A further word of warning: don't attempt it if either of you is suffering from haemorrhoids or depression. Your best hope, in fact, is that this ridiculous book will put you off sex for life, in which case the fact that you're not getting your greens will no longer irk you.

Good luck!

Yours,

Emma Jane

Dear Emma Jane,

Thank you so much for your kind letter. I bought a copy of The Joy of Sex, *as you suggested, locked up the Jack Russell, postponed a meeting of the Tenants' Association, cancelled the milk and the morning papers, cleared a working area in the garage 25ft by 18ft and got cracking. It was no good. After two days my husband had still failed to get an erection and look where we are now.*

Frustrated,
The Casualty Ward,
St Mark's Hospital,
Ryde,
Isle of Wight

Dear Frustrated,

Oh my! Tell me, how old are you and your husband?

Yours,

Emma Jane

Dear Emma Jane,

> *My husband's 79 but I'm only 76.*
> *Frustrated,*
> *The Casualty Ward,*
> *St Mark's Hospital,*
> *Ryde,*
> *Isle of Wight*

Dear Frustrated,

> 79 and 76? Bloody Norah! When did your husband stop showing an interest in the physical side of marriage?
> > Yours,
> > Emma Jane

Dear Emma Jane,

> *On the Monday night before I first wrote to you and again on Tuesday morning.*
> > *Still Frustrated,*
> > *Alex Comfort Rest Home,*
> > *Shanklin,*
> > *Isle of Wight*

Darling Polly,

> Here, Jill Tweedie took me out to lunch at Bianchi's yesterday. She's writing an article for *The Guardian* on immorality,[30] so of course she had to come up to the sharp end for some hard information. She got me as pissed as a pudding and I blew the whistle on nearly everyone, including you, I'm sorry to say. She particularly liked my story of the time you absent-mindedly left the Minister of Arts hanging

63

upside-down in your wardrobe for twenty-four hours like a garlic sausage in a German delicatessen. She says that when I at last hand in my badge I should start a business advising sexologists — a sexologists' sexologist, as it were. I must say they need one.

My new friend, Dr Bryson from Warwick University, has been staying for a few days and he's lovely. Over dinner last night he said: "If I could have my life over again I'd like Malcolm Muggeridge to have been a monk." Nice? And he's a splendid person to watch television with. At one point he suddenly became very agitated and said: "Here, I do hope we're not missing anything bad on the other channel." And he meant it. He's a particular student of Quinn Martin Productions. Over in L.A. you must get them all night long. What bliss! Anyway, on Monday he took me to a meeting of the Aristotelian Society, where Dr Barrie Paskins read a paper on "Some Victims of Morality".[31] Not bad though it seemed to me to lean rather heavily on Bernard Williams's now celebrated trap.[32] Anyway, what would a philosopher know from morality? That's my department and I caused a bit of a stir at question time by saying as much. Anthony *"Cannon* should be compulsory viewing for all fat men" Quinton in the chair. Very urbane. Wears suede shoes and smokes Players, you know the type. Wouldn't be surprised if he cropped up one day on *Celebrity Squares*. For his summing-up contribution he scored a mere twenty-two on the clapometer. Nine for presentation (he is witty), eight for star quality, but only five for content. Do you remember how, in the grim days of *Sunday Night at the London Palladium*, some palsied droll lately discovered down a pit by Lew Grade only had to say the magic words "Harold Wilson" or "Ted

Heath" to bring the house down? Well, interestingly enough, philosophical turns also have stand-by catch phrases that seem to go straight to the collective funny bone. A speaker only has to smile mischievously and say "Economist!" or "Sociologist!" to have little old philosophers clutching their ribs and rolling in the aisles.

Last Wednesday I went with Dawn Upstairs, Black Danielle and Pretty Marie to entertain the ******** Brothers and a mixed bag of pop stars and disc jockeys. When I got home, the old boy was highly insulting. He claimed not to understand why desirable pop stars would pay the likes of me and Dawn Upstairs to get up to immorality with them. "If they showed their faces in a club," he said, "they'd be knocked down in the rush. In fact they'd gather enough little groupies to last them for a week. No offence meant, my dear, but it doesn't make sense." As it happens, it makes a great deal of sense, as you and I well know, and as I painstakingly tried to point out to the silly old sausage. Unlike groupies, we professional ladies do as we're told, stand on our heads, go this that and the other way without calling anyone a deviant, smile bravely while suppressing murderous thoughts, leave as soon as the mini-cab arrives, and, what's more, *without* our benefactors' credit cards, travellers' cheques, astrological med-allions, cuff-links, Cartier watches and expensive new camera systems stuffed into our handbags. Right? Nor are we likely to give them the clap, sell our experiences to pornographic journals such as *The News of the World* or put the squeeze on them the next day by saying we're pregnant. Good gracious, if I were a rock and roll singer I'd book me and cut out the aggravation. Wouldn't you? The old boy isn't too quick on the uptake these days, but I think he got the general picture after a while. Anyway, he shut up. Then, over tea today, Dawn Upstairs and I tried to explain to him how much *nicer* women are than men. Men, we argued, had not the slightest compunction about going to bed with married women, but the majority of women will not treat with a married man, identifying strongly with the poor little wife at home, up to her elbows in the week's wash. Of course Dawn Upstairs and I insisted that this rule held for us. "Unless there's £30 on the table," said the old boy with a cynical sneer, imagining, I suppose, that he was making a devastating debating point. As usual, of course, the poor old fruit was up a gum tree. We explained — very slowly, as though interpreting a street map for a foreigner — how by attending to the needs of randy married men, we were saving them from the clutches of greedy temporary secretaries and other ambitious amateurs who *would* pose a threat to family life. "Absolutely right!" said Dawn Upstairs, and off she trotted to continue the affair she's having with a married man she met down Annabel's last week. She is a disappointment sometimes.

> Lots of love,
> Emma Jane

Dear Emma Jane,
> *Do you know Linda Lovelace?*
> *Interested,*
> *Belgrave Square, S.W.3.*

Dear Interested,

I've met Linda like socially and I can tell you she's a sweet natural girl with an infectious sense of fun. I think I should warn you, however, that the practice for which she's become famous can be dangerous. I said as much to Linda when I met her last summer at Royal Ascot, but she said she wasn't bothered. Over strawberries and cream in the tea-tent, she explained that she came from a long line of dare-devils, many of whom had lost their lives in accidents. It is not generally known, for instance, that her grandmother went down on the *Titanic*.

> Love,
> Emma Jane

✻   ✻   ✻

The Rt Hon. Lord Longford PC,
Sidgwick & Jackson Ltd, London, W.C.1.

Dear Lord Longford,

    I have recently completed a study of invest-igative journalists. My hypothesis is that — notwith-standing at which end of the market they ply their trade — they are human beings like the rest of us (their eyes tell us this), owing their low standing in society more to misfortunes in the past than to any unifying moral deformity. My method has been recklessly un-Popperian in that I have generalised from observed instances.

    I wonder whether your firm might care to read it with a view to publication?

> Yours sincerely,
> Emma Jane Crampton

Dear Miss Crampton,

    Lord Longford is away, but he has asked me to write and thank you for your letter about your interesting idea of a book on investigative journalists.

This has been discussed with our editorial staff who alas! do not feel that we could make a commercial success of it here.

We hope that you will find another publisher who is more enterprising.

Yours sincerely,
Gwendolen Keeble,
Private Secretary to Lord Longford

❋   ❋   ❋

Emma Jane, love, at a recent wine and cheese get-together of Women in the Media we decided to carry out an across-the-board analysis of viable sexual attitudes prevalent among kids in socio-biological-economic sub-groups C3 and D1 and their bearing on fundamental human relationships in the sample area. At the end of the day we wanted to know whether aggression is merely depression turned outwards, as is now thought to be the case, or whether, in fact, the reverse is true. We therefore ran in groups of three into various pubs in the Islington area with carrots up our noses and handed round copies of Professor T.S. Fzuszs's "S.Q." (or "Sex Quotient") tests which he has devised after many years of fruitful work with rats. Due to an unforeseeable show of what field psychologists now call "compensatory guilt displacement activity" (i.e. cries of "Buzz off you silly old crow, can't you see I'm chatting up my bird?" etc.) we were unable to arrive at a subjectively valid analysis of the problem; but we were able to corroborate Professor Fzuszs's findings re the attitude of rats to being given

electric shocks. I enclose a copy of our report and
very much look forward to hearing your reactions.

> *Yours,*
> *Anna Raeburn,*
> *Sexology Unit,*
> *Women in the Media*

Dear Anna,

Many thanks for sending me a copy of your working party's report on imperfectly socialised responses in the sample area. I must say I've always been under the impression that kids are young goats, but we live and learn. On the whole, the report confirms my belief that while men are conditioned to behave like superior imitations of women they will never attain their true potential as *men*, nor take their rightful place in a caring society.

As it happens, I bought a copy of Professor Fzuszs's *Test Your Own S.Q.* (Pelican £1.75) only last week, and was much stimulated by the Professor's many challenging assertions. I was particularly impressed by the wealth of evidence he musters to support his controversial theory that the comparative failure of non-Caucasians to compete successfully with Caucasians in advanced industrial societies can be entirely attributed to the abnormally high S.Q. to be found in non-Caucasian males. As you will know, the Professor's work is causing a great stir in learned circles due to its bearing on the "nature versus nurture" debate, and has already achieved a degree of Modern Masterdom thanks to exposure in *The Sunday Times Colour Supplement* and on a recent five-hour BBC2 spectacular ("Science in a Nutshell") entertainingly compered by Ritchie Benaud and Diana Rigg, in which the emphasis was on the Professor's exciting theory that S.Q. is 89% due to genetic factors and only 11% to environment.

The tests devised by Professor Fzuszs to enable one to measure one's own S.Q. were extremely interesting, though I must admit they produced some disconcerting results in my own household. My young man would seem not to have an S.Q. at all, I have one of only 49, but my girlfriend Big Elaine turns out to have one of 168, which, according to Fzuszs's chart, means she should be a deck-hand on a Norwegian whaler or in the fiddle section of the London Symphony Orchestra. Her answer to one of the questions ("Insert the bottle in one of the squares below", I think it was) carries, if I'm not mistaken, a maximum sentence of fifteen years.

Keep up the good work, and *do* write to me if you have any more nasty problems like that last one.

Yours,
Emma Jane [33]

❊ ❊ ❊

Dear Mrs Windrush,

Get a handyman to fix it securely, that's my advice to you. We changed ours for an old-fashioned wooden one not long ago, but we failed to screw it on tightly enough. Sitting there peacefully one morning doing the *Guardian* crossword, Toby Danvers the Impresario aimed a kick at the cat and shot feet first out of the door and down the stairs like a tobogganist on the Cresta Run. He'd have been out of the front door and down the street if his rupture belt hadn't got caught in the banisters.

Yours,
Emma Jane

Dear Emma Jane,

In Both the Ladies and the Gentlemen, *there is a passage in which Nigel of British Intelligence has fantasies about you and Aylesbury Yvonne "going the other way". My flatmate Janet and I are eager to try this, but we are not quite sure what the expression means. Can you explain?*

> *Yours sincerely,*
> *J.W.K. Bright (Ms),*
> *King's Road, S.W.3.*

Dear Ms Bright,

I certainly can, and it's fortunate indeed that you live in the King's Road, where this sort of thing is looked upon as absolutely normal. To avoid the tourists, however, I suggest that you and Janet get up very early one morning, dress in warm clothes and sally forth together while the streets are still deserted. Once outside your flat wave goodbye to Janet and walk in an easterly direction towards Sloane Square. Janet meanwhile should march off in a westerly direction towards the Co-op at World's End. If you carry out this manoeuvre correctly it could fairly be said that she will be "going the other way". Relative to her, of course, *you* will be "going the other way". Relative to the milkman proceeding north towards the Fulham Road, you will both be "going the other way", though not as yet together. That manoeuvre is much more complicated and will take another letter. As Wittgenstein wrote to Russell in 1914: "Doesn't the principle of sufficient reason say simply that space and time are relative? I now think that this is quite obvious, because all events which, according to this assertion, are not meant to be possible could only occur, if at all, in an absolute time and space.

But think of the case of the particle that is the only thing existing in the world and that has been at rest for all eternity and that suddenly, at time A, begins to move. Think of this and similar cases and you will see, I believe, that it is *not* an *a priori* insight that makes such events seem impossible to us *unless it is the case* that space and time are relative." (My translation from the original German.) [34] None of which is to say, of course, that Relativity theory predicts the possibility of going backwards in time. The popular rhyme:

> There was a young lady called Bright
> Who could travel faster than light.
> She set out one day
> In a relative way
> And returned the previous night

is formally incoherent in that it breaks the law of contradiction. Unless, that is, you don't exist, in which case you fall outside the range of this particular law, in that any quality at all can be predicated of you, including that of being in two places at once.

> With very best wishes to you and Janet,
> Love,
> Emma Jane

Darling Polly,

No, of *course* I haven't told anyone about you and George Burns, and, for the last time, *I'm not publishing any of your letters*. Mind you, the top houses are beating a path to my door. The Oxford University Press have been particularly eager, but in the end I preferred Eyre Methuen. Slightly more class, I felt. What's good enough for Lord Blake and Babar the Elephant is good enough for me. When the deal was done I said to Dawn Upstairs: "Eyre Methuen's taken my book." "Oooh," she said, "who's he? A burglar?" Some people you can't impress.

Here, Kathleen Tynan rang up the old boy last night and asked him to introduce her to a lesbian. The silly old coot nearly fell over backwards with excitement. Well, you know how he is. She's rewriting the Bianca Jagger film, it seems, and she needs some hard information for a naughty scene. He's taking Dawn Upstairs along to meet Mrs T tomorrow. That's ridiculous. She's no more bisexual than me. Which isn't saying much I suppose 'cos I am. And so's she, come to that. Oh well. The old fool wants to take the sauna bath door along with him. He's in a tremendous state of excitement and I have to keep reminding him that it's a literary meeting, no more, no less. I do hope he isn't going to let me down.

On Tuesday I had dinner at the Junior Carlton with One-Eyed Charlie and my new friend Auberon Waugh.[35] Since One-Eyed Charlie is only at ease with people who are so clever that their brains are actually sticking out of their heads, I was afraid he'd become bored in such company; but on the whole he behaved beautifully. The only tricky moment occurred right at the start, when One-Eyed Charlie, confusing Bron with Richard Afton of *The Evening News* — an easy mistake to make, I suppose — congratulated him on his witty television column. Bron angrily pretended not to know what television was, but One-Eyed Charlie managed to cheer him up with a pleasant story about Ryle's unswerving philistinism. Stop me if you've heard it. Some years ago, it seems, Ryle and Isaiah Berlin both happened to be in Cambridge one evening: Ryle to call on Broad and

Berlin to attend a performance of Bach's B minor Mass in King's chapel. Meeting unexpectedly in King's Parade, Ryle said: "You been listening to tunes again, Isaiah?" Bron chuckled at this anecdote — while protesting in his bluff way, of course, that he'd heard of none of the people involved — and then he invited me and the old boy to be his guests at Combe Florey towards the end of September. Bron's a bit of an old buffer and I'm not sure I'd like the pig-sticking expeditions I'm told he organises for his visitors, but I think we may go because the other guests sound quite cranky: George Gale, Lord and Lady Weidenfeld, Mr and Mrs Stoat [36] and something called Mad Mitch. On the way home, One-Eyed Charlie said: "He's really not a bad conversationalist for someone who spends his whole time not watching television." One-Eyed Charlie's a terrible snob, of course, and he pretends to watch everything; but I know for a fact that he only likes the funny programmes: *Fawlty Towers, Porridge, Dad's Army* and *The Sweeney*.

Then on Wednesday Julian Mitchell came to dinner. (How am I doing any work, you must be wondering. I'm not. Realising that only industrial action on my part will make the old boy pull his finger out, I've been on an unofficial go-slow for the last ten days.) Anyway, I'd scarcely served the fish before Julian threw himself into an unprovoked attack on, of all people, Clive James. He didn't pick up any points for that in *this* household, I can tell you. Good heavens. He said Clive wasn't a serious television critic. A serious *literary* critic, yes, but in his *Observer* hat merely frivolous, ignoring first-rate work and reviewing only piffle that allowed him to be witty. Who then was a serious TV critic? Only Dennis Potter, we eventually agreed, though we had certain reservations about some of his own plays. What a lark it is when cultivated people meet over a civilised dinner table! I see myself as the last of the old-fashioned literary hostesses — a successor to Viva King, no less. At one point Julian said: "Les Dawson may not be a great comedian, but he's certainly another Tony Hancock." Rather a good left and right on two absurdly inflated reputations, don't you think? I fancy him no end, as it happens (Julian, that is, not Les Dawson), but this shall remain a secret between you and me. It is my misfortune, as you know, to be turned on only by men who choose their words carefully. After dinner, he suddenly said to the old boy, out of the blue and apropos of nothing at all: "When you were in the Navy did you purposely keep your weight down in the hope that you'd be accepted on demobilisation by the Royal Ballet School?" Talk about a conversational Pearl Harbor! The old boy was well scattered, I can tell you. The two of them then exchanged boring reminiscences about their years in submarines. The extent to which these arty types are emotionally hung up on their more manly pasts is really quite extraordinary.

> Tons of love,
> Emma Jane

Dear Emma Jane,

A few years ago, that fine artiste Michael Denison and his gracious wife Dulcie Grey stayed for a few days in Pontypridd while filming in this part of the world. They did us the great honour of attending a local dance and their demeanour towards us ordinary folk was so friendly, informal and natural that it quite made our evening. From their behaviour you'd

have thought they were just the same as you or I.
          Betty Pond (Mrs)
          Mountain Ash, Glamorgan

Dear Mrs Pond,

          You were lucky, believe me. When they were in our neck of the woods, they kicked down the front door, tipped my little old granny head-first into the tumble-dryer, gave the cat an enema, set fire to the Filipino au pair boy and left without so much as a "Thank you very much" or "You must come round to our place some time." [37]
          Yours,
          Emma Jane

Dear Emma Jane,

          I need your advice. My husband and I are an ordinary couple who have been happily married for nine years. Recently, however, he has taken to reading Men Only *and* Curious, *entering* The Sun's *"Guilty Pleasures" competition, sticking the same paper's saucy Page 3 lovelies on the wall of his do-it-yourself room, neglecting his whippet, ignoring his homework, letting the Black and Decker drill I bought him for Christmas lie idle and coming home as late as 6.30 on a Friday night. He says he still loves me, that I am flesh and blood, whereas the shameless magazine girls are mere harmless shadows, but I'm afraid he's become a victim of the permissive society. What can I do?*

          Yours sincerely,
          Ethel Putts,
          Ealing

Dear Mrs Putts,

          You're right to be concerned. Being weak-willed and easily led, men have to be supervised every minute of the day for their own good. So-called experts in the psychology of siege relationships advise participants to establish an atmosphere of trust and confidence, but as far as I'm concerned a "pairing situation", as it's now called, is all about who carries the gun. Your fight, in fact, is against the cowardly bullies who, for fat profits, are putting temptation in your husband's path. Pornography is a drug and, as happens to all who take drugs, the slide into the gutter is slow but sure. A taste for soft drugs leads, as we know, to a craving for the harder stuff, and this habit, once acquired, leads inevitably to ... no! I can't even bring myself to put the words on paper. You must act at once. Immoral pictures breed immoral thoughts and immoral thoughts lead, in spite of your husband's ignorant protestations to the contrary, to immoral deeds. You must stop him thinking the unthinkable, and to this end all erotic material must be banished from the family home. This may seem harsh, but the distance between thought and action is shorter, I think you will agree, than that between thinking and not thinking. "Justice must tame whom mercy fails to train," as Judge Buzzard is wont to say to a man he's about to pop in the pokey for twenty years.

If this doesn't work, plenty of exercise might be the answer. Persuade him to run three miles every morning and three more every evening. By the end of the week the cheeky monkey will be forty-two miles away and someone else's problem.

Be Firm! The Women's Movement are watching you!
Yours,
Emma Jane

Dear Ms Stassinopoulos,

Yes I did indeed glance through Ms Bel Mooney's article in *The Daily Express* about the delights of open marriage, but I'm afraid I found it predictably wrong-headed. "Open marriage" as a concept seems to me to embody a contradiction of the order of "free-lance under exclusive contract". To assert, as Ms Mooney does, that one is in favour of a contradiction is to assert everything and nothing. A pupil of Duns Scotus (without making use of a formal calculus, incidentally) conclusively proved that from a contradiction any statement whatsoever can be validly derived. Allow me to demonstrate. First take any contradiction. I suggest the conjunction of the two propositions: (1) "Ms Bel Mooney is a sexologist" and (2) "Ms Bel Mooney is not a sexologist". Now take any false proposition. I suggest "Pigs fly". Next take one half of the initial contradiction as a separate premise. From "Ms Bel Mooney is a sexologist" it certainly follows that "Ms Bel Mooney is a sexologist" and/or "Pigs fly". For given that x is true, whatever x may be, it follows necessarily for the same value of x and for any value of y, that x and/or y is true. Next we take the second half of the initial contradiction: (2) "Ms Bel Mooney is not a sexologist". Taking our previous conclusion as one premise and this as the other, we necessarily arrive at our pleasantly false conclusion. Thus:

"Ms Bel Mooney is a sexologist and/or pigs fly."

"Ms Bel Mooney is not a sexologist."

Therefore "Pigs fly."

I have demonstrated, I think, that to commit yourself to asserting a contradiction is, even for a sexologist, to commit yourself to asserting anything at all that it is possible to assert and also, of course, to its denial. Marriage is a formal order and to start complaining even as the jaws of the marriage vows close around you is on all fours with complaining against the off-side rule in soccer. If you don't like the conventions, don't play. Cheer up, though, and remember that marriage is a necessary condition of divorce.[38]

> Yours,
> Emma Jane

Dear Emma Jane,

I'm keen to go on holiday to Majorca with my girlfriend from the office, but to do this I will have to raise a personal loan. I've just heard that fringe bankers and such-like usurers have been known to lend money to young girls and then agree to cancel the debt if they will submit to acts of gross intimacy. Can this be true?

> *Yours,*
> *Antoinette Appleby,*
> *Camberley, Surrey*

Dear Antoinette,

Yes, I'm afraid there's some truth in the horrifying stories you've heard. I know this for a fact because my friend Pretty Marie called on just such an unscrupulous bank manager not long ago. "Now look here," she said, "I'm Pretty Marie, me, and I hear that you lend money to young girls and then, when they can't pay it back, you threaten to ruin them unless they submit their bodies to your foul desires." "Ah well," said the bank manager, "I dare say such dreadful things have been known to happen, but I'm sure . . ." "Good," said Pretty Marie, "in that case I'd like to borrow £15,000." She got the money and now she's going to try the National Westminster.

With best wishes,

Yours,

Emma Jane

Dear Miss Emma Jane,

Forgive me, but if a gentleman caller such as myself were to visit your block of flats, am I not right in thinking that he would have to choose between you, Big Elaine and Dawn Upstairs. Wouldn't he be better advised to stick to Shepherd's Market where he could have his pick of at least fifty lovely young models? Most is best, that's my philosophy.

Yours sincerely,

Horatio Putts,

Ealing

Dear Horatio,

Is it really? Well, I've got news for you. When a mug visits this block of flats, he hasn't got only three choices, as you mistakenly assert — me, Big Elaine and Dawn Upstairs — he has eight choices. Great heavens, did Cantor live in vain? A class of n terms has, as every school-boy knows, $2n$ sub-classes. Big Elaine, Dawn Upstairs and I constitute a class of three, I think you will agree, and we therefore contain eight sub-classes (or choices open to the gentleman caller). These are: (1) all three of us, (2) Dawn Upstairs, (3) Big Elaine, (4) Me, (5) Big Elaine and Dawn Upstairs, (6) Big Elaine and me, (7) Dawn Upstairs and me, and (8) none of us. If Pretty Marie moved into the block (which God forbid) he'd have sixteen choices (2 to the power of 4). If you don't believe me, work it out. Cantor proved, incidentally, that when n is infinite, $2n$ is greater than n. It follows from this that there are more classes of things than there are things. Therefore classes are not things. From this it follows that there are fewer things in heaven and earth, Horatio, than are dreamt of in your philosophy. So stick to Shepherd's Market and leave me out.

> Love,
> Emma Jane

Dear Emma Jane,

> *I'm against all forms of censorship and feel that it was wrong of the Queen to intervene in the matter of Jens Thorsen's proposed film about Christ. Don't you agree?*

> > *Yours sincerely,*
> > *Arnold Goodman,* [39]
> > *Essex Street, London.*

Dear Lord Goodman,

> No I don't. What would happen if *everyone* made a pornographic film about Christ? A clinching argument, I think you'll admit. Well done Ma'am! that's what I say.

> > Yours sincerely,
> > Emma Jane Crampton

Dear Emma Jane,

> *Thank you for your letter of the 21st but the "what would happen if everyone . . . " argument is not as clinching as you would wish. Consider the case of the extreme utilitarian who lives in a society in*

which every member reasons as he does. Should such a person make a pornographic film about Christ if so minded? As a first approximation I agree with you that he should not. Since the situation is a completely symmetrical one, what is rational for him is rational for others. Hence, by a reductio ad absurdum *argument it would seem that making a pornographic film about Christ would be rational for none. Nevertheless, and with respect, I would point out that a rather more refined analysis shows that this argument is not quite correct, though it is correct enough for most practical purposes. The argument considers each person as confronted with the choice either of making a pornographic film about Christ or of not doing so. However, there is a third possibility, which is that each person should, with the aid of a randomising device, such as a throwing dice, give himself a certain probability of making a pornographic film about Christ. This would be to adopt what in the theory of games is called a "mixed strategy". Were we to give numerical values to the private benefit of making pornographic films about Christ and to the public harm done by 1, 2, 3 etc. persons making such films, we could work out a value of the probability of making a pornographic film about Christ that each extreme utilitarian should give himself. Let* a *be the value which each extreme utilitarian gets from making a pornographic film about Christ, and let* $f(1)$, $f(2)$, $f(3)$ *etc. be the public harm done by exactly 1, 2, 3 etc. persons respectively making pornographic films about Christ. Suppose that* p *is the probability that each person gives himself of making a pornographic film about Christ. Then we can easily calculate, as functions of* p, *the probabilities that 1, 2, 3 etc. persons will make pornographic films about Christ. Let these probabilities*

*be p1, p2, . . . pn. Then the total net probable benefit
can be expressed as:*

V = p1(a−f(1) + p2(2a−f(2)) + . . . pn(na−f(n))
Then if we know the function f(x) *we can calculate
the value of* p *for which* (dV/dp) = 0. *This gives the
value of* p *which it would be rational for each extreme
utilitarian to adopt.*

*I have demonstrated, I think you will agree,
that "everybody does* x*" and "nobody does* x*" are not,
as is often assumed, the only relevant and symmetrical
alternatives. So stick that on your knitting needles
and knit it, clever clogs.*

> *Yours sincerely,*
> *Arnold Goodman*

Dear Emma Jane,

*Isn't your job rather dangerous? Don't your
clients ever become violent?*

> *Concerned,*
> *Worthing*

Dear Concerned,

Not really. In fact I've only been caught up
in three really hairy situations since taking up the
way of life. The first was with an eminent Q.C. who
coached the Oxford Boat Race crew for many years
(including the year they sneakily rowed ten men and
sank), but who now prefers to dress up as Petunia
Clark the *chanteuse* and chase you round the room
with a number four iron. The second, and even more
distasteful, experience was with a sadistic base metal
merchant who ties you up and makes you watch a
video tape of Michael Parkinson sucking up to David
Niven — no one will visit *him* a second time, I can tell

you. The third, and worst of all, was a case of indecent assault and attempted rape involving my girlfriend Big Elaine and three drill sergeants from the Parachute Regiment, on leave from Northern Ireland. Golly Moses what a ruck! I was so frightened I called in six tear-arses from Chelsea Police Station to restore order. Fortunately for my girlfriend Big Elaine, we were able to persuade the drill sergeants not to prosecute.

> Yours,
> Emma Jane

Dear Emma Jane,

> *I recently read a letter in* Penthouse *from a man who said he "dressed the wrong way". I'm frightened that I too might suffer from this complaint, but I can't discover what the expression means. Is it dangerous? I'm getting married in the near future.*
>
> *Yours,*
> *Distraught,*
> *Barnstaple*

Dear Distraught,

> Thank you for your letter. "Dressing the wrong way" is to be avoided at all costs. As applied to a man, it means that when getting dressed in the morning he is careless enough to put his boxer shorts on back to front, with disastrous consequences, as the following cautionary tale will illustrate. My friend One-Eyed Charlie dressed the wrong way one morning, but was unaware of the fact until he found himself caught short in the West End. Upon attempting to make use of the public convenience situated in Piccadilly Underground Station, he discovered that in order to relieve himself with any degree of comfort,

84

he was compelled to adopt the unusual procedure in this situation of lowering his trousers and boxer shorts to the level of his knees. This he did, whereupon he was immediately the object of indecent advances from thirteen plain clothes detectives disguised as homosexual Russian agents and Chinese dope fiends. He told them to "get on their bikes" and was promptly arrested for abusive behaviour and marched off to West End Central. Here, armed with two offensive weapons — namely his kidneys — he was hot-headed enough to assault all thirteen. He was charged with indecent exposure against Her Majesty's peace and with GBH against half the Morals Squad. He drew six months in the boob, so let it be a lesson to you. Be careful how you dress in the morning.

> Yours,
> Emma Jane

Darling Polly,

Well, it was Monty's funeral yesterday, but at the last minute the old boy refused to attend out of some obscure sense of loyalty to the Auk. We gave our tickets to Black Danielle and One-Eyed Charlie. I stayed at home, but the old boy paraded up and down the Fulham Road with a banner saying: "The Battle of El Alamein was won by Field-Marshal Sir Claude Auchinleck — OK?" An enraged little Desert Rat, who happened to be hobbling past, punched him up the nose and chased him all the way home. He must have been ninety, but he looked older. I saw the little bugger off, I can tell you.

Hey, guess what, I'm an authority at last! Not yet in the class of Ms Anna "viable human beings"

Raeburn, to be sure, but an authority nevertheless. This morning a nicely spoken lady from *The Observer* rang me up and said they were asking certain well-connected people whether they were in favour of state-controlled brothels. That old thing, right? Would I care to give an opinion? I'd be only too pleased, I said, and I quickly polished up the following sensible statement: "I'm against state-controlled brothels for the same reason that Robert Frost was against free verse. It would be like playing tennis without a net. Making brothels legal would remove half the fun and anyway we've got to give The Hammer of the Yard a run for his money." [40] What do you think? Nice one Emma Jane? Then, reluctant to be left out of the fun, I suppose, *The Sunday Telegraph* sent a charming young reporter called Anthony Haden-Guest round to the flat to interview me about my forthcoming collection of letters. My pal Dr Bryson, up for the day from Warwick, insisted on being present. "Never grant the press an interview," he said, "unless accompanied by your philosopher. If he becomes impertinent I'll clap him in a paradox." In the circumstances, the interview went very smoothly, as you can see from the enclosed photographs. (Henri insisted on being present too.)

These small flourishes notwithstanding, I was later thrown into a black depression by inadvertantly watching Shirley MacLaine chatting vivaciously to Russell Harty on TV. At one point, she gave Russell a most moving account of how, as part of the preparation for her role in *Irma La Douce*, she had lived for a short time among the prostitutes of Paris. And what do you know! Under their hard exteriors, Russell, these prostitutes were just like you or me — *viable* human beings with the same hopes, fears and problems as the rest of us. Dear God, as if our calling wasn't bad enough without some half-witted mime following us around with a notebook and Japanese tape-recorder! I've written to her c/o the London Palladium, where she's currently doing a turn, and now I feel slightly better.

I'd feel better still if you'd come back to London.

Lots of love,
Emma Jane

✻　✻　✻

Dear Miss MacLaine,

I am a prostitute and in the course of my work I am sometimes called upon to play the part of an actress. If, while you are in London, you would allow me to spend a certain amount of time in your company, I feel I could thereafter more realistically simulate for my clients' benefit a mime's grotesque vanity, her herculean stupidity and her offensive patronising of her superiors. I might even discover that under the artificial gush and clatter an actress is a real human being, more deserving of our sympathy than our condemnation. I look forward to hearing from you.

With best wishes,
Yours sincerely,
Emma Jane Crampton

Notes by William Donaldson

This collection of letters is such an odd blend of truth and what Emma Jane would no doubt call "the higher truth" that on reading it in proof I immediately protested to her publishers. They have very properly allowed me to add here some brief interpretative notes to alert the credulous.

1. Motor Show Polly. A close friend of Emma Jane's, her cognomen is a tribute to her annual decorative appearances on the British Leyland stand at Earl's Court. In the summer of 1976 she moved her business to Los Angeles, where it has flourished.

2. This reference to John from the North's politics has to do, I imagine, with the fact that he's an old-style, slapstick Tory who has repeatedly offered himself to the electorate (happily with no success) on an uncomplicated "Bring back flogging and hanging" platform. Pretty Marie once observed, not altogether originally, that if he were any further to the right he'd be in the North Sea. In some quarters he is thought to be making a bid to be the next Tory intellectual after Lord Hailsham.

3. The suggestion here that Emma Jane was locked in the bedroom against her will throughout Alan Brien's visit is misleading. At this period she lived in constant fear of being exposed by the popular press and in fact it was *her* decision to remain concealed in the bedroom until Mr Brien had gone. Some months after this incident, she decided to "come out", as it were, and, as this slim volume testifies, clamber belatedly aboard the bandwagon.

4. I take this to be a joke of some sort. I cerainly don't recall such an incident, and I don't go out very much.

5. This passage is wildly fanciful. My representations to Miss Marrian were perfectly proper — directed through her agent and more or less under my own name — and it was my intention merely to take strikingly original photographs of this excellent model. In this I was entirely successful. (*See* Advertisement.) I did not at this or any other time call myself Henri Le Branleur.

6. To save her mother needless distress, Emma Jane has been obliged over the years to invent various employments

for herself, in order to explain her relatively comfortable life-style. At this time, she had, in her imagination, just been dismissed by Mr Georg Solti for some confusion with the band parts, and had gone to work twice a week for Mr Previn.

7. I doubt whether Clive James said this to Emma Jane, since it doesn't seem to be exactly his style.

8. Emma Jane seems to be in the toil of some private grievance against the police in general and Sir Robert Mark in particular. This puzzles me. Hanging above the desk in her study, she has a charming photograph of Sir Robert, signed by himself and containing a warm assurance of his best wishes. This had always led me to suppose that they were on the most cordial terms. (*See* Advertisement.)

9. The photographs of Emma Jane and Nigel Dempster are not as compromising as she would perhaps like the reader to suppose. They are, however, items for the connoisseur. (*See* Advertisement.)

10. The account of my photographing British Intelligence from the wardrobe is not entirely accurate. I wasn't in the wardrobe but behind the bedroom curtains, from which vantage point I was able to take some telling investigative photographs. (*See* Advertisement.) Dawn Upstairs, who has a key to the flat and is thus able to use it as though it were her own, or even ours, happened to walk into the room at a particularly sensitive moment. It was then that British Intelligence said: "Ah, good to see you 006. Damn clever disguise, if I may say so." I remained concealed throughout.

11. PUSSI is a serious organisation and it ill behoves Emma Jane to sneer at it in this way. Similarly, I find the jocular and no doubt intentionally hurtful reference to Jeremy Sandford somewhat offensive.

12. In this letter Emma Jane, a staunch ontological individualist, is making an important point, for once, and it's a pity, perhaps, that either she or her publishers didn't find room to quote at greater length from Mr Maudling's strange article in *The Times*. It might have been appropriate, also, to have referred to Anthony Quinton's paper on Social Objects (see *The Proceedings of The Aristotelian Society*, 97th Session, page 13) in which he quotes McTaggart's telling remark: "Compared with the worship of the State, zoolatry is rational and dignified. A bull or a crocodile may not have great intrinsic value, but it has some, for it is a conscious being.

The State has none. It would be as reasonable to worship a sewage-pipe, which also possesses considerable value as means." The phrase "bloated universe" is happy, but not, alas, original. Quine uses it in his celebrated paper *On What There Is* (*From a Logical Point of View*, Harper and Row, 1953), but since Emma Jane has almost certainly not read this important article, we can perhaps conclude that the borrowing is accidental.

13. This incident, while not as wilfully misreported as the first involving Miss Marrian, still manages to convey a false impression. It was regrettably the case that I had not yet paid Miss Marrian and, further, that she had been compelled to make polite representation to Emma Jane by post re the matter of her outstanding account. It is not true, however, that Emma Jane had to pay her. She gave me the money and I paid her. The rest of the passage is more or less accurate and the photographs that Miss Marrian agreed to pose for are among the most unusual I have taken. (*See* Advertisement.)

14. It seems to me probable that Emma Jane wrote to Miss Claire Raynor with the sole intention of eliciting a foolish reply, which would enable her to hold this caring sexologist up to ridicule. I find such trickery rather distasteful and it pleases me, therefore, that thanks to Miss Raynor's extremely sensible letter it is Emma Jane who ends up looking foolish.

15. I think Emma Jane is being needlessly harsh with Mrs Chobham. Kinsey drew attention to the fact that "lesbian contacts have been observed in such widely separated species as rats, mice, hamsters, guinea pigs, rabbits, porcupines, marten, cattle, antelope, goats, horses, pigs, lions, sheep, monkey and hippopotomuses." Kinsey *et al, Sexual Behaviour in the Human Female* (New York: Pocket Books, 1965). It might have been comforting for Mrs Chobham to know that she and her friend Margaret were in such good company.

16. It is true that Big Elaine kept a leopard for a time, but fortunately the only person it bit was Big Elaine's mother, so no damage was done. As far as I can discover there is no Mayor of West Hampstead, so this must be one of Emma Jane's jokes. Meanwhile, Miss Joyce is still waiting for some sensible advice. Typical.

17. Emma Jane cannot possibly have taken this pornographic letter to be the work of *Forum*'s urbane editor, Phillip Hodson. I fail to understand why she thought it would be

amusing to attribute it to him.

18. Nice one Esther! It was not to be foreseen, I think, that the saucy punster would, with a fractional shift of her considerable weight, squash Emma Jane as flat as a dab and in the process give her a salutary lesson in good manners.

18. Why this gratuitous insult to Mrs Conran? I am not aware of her ever having made any literary claims for herself, and she writes, as far as I can tell, just as well as the next cook. How would Emma Jane feel if, in the course of reviewing this book for *House and Garden*, say, Mrs Conran made slighting reference to Emma Jane's shortcomings in the field of domestic science?

20. F.R. Leavis, *The Clark Lectures*, 1967 (Chatto and Windus, 1969).

21. Emma Jane thoroughly deserved the elegant rap across the knuckles administered by Mr Tynan in his kind preface, of course, but the rest of this passage is, surprisingly, more or less accurate. True Mr Tynan had no occasion to tell young Amis to take his elbows off the table, but Emma Jane's account of her early exit from the party is all too true alas. Imagine my mortification when she suddenly rose to her feet (interrupting Mrs Gilliatt in mid-anecdote, if I'm not mistaken), to inform these distinguished literary people that she had to "go and do my thing with two mugs and Dawn Upstairs". It is not surprising, perhaps, that we have not been invited to another of these glittering occasions.

22. I take this to be another of Emma Jane's jokes. If she received such a letter, I think we can assume it came from some prankster, not from Mr Ingrams. They've met only once, as far as I know, at a *Private Eye* charity rag, the purpose of which I've forgotten, but at which she'd agreed to make a fund-raising appearance — and on that occasion he treated her with the utmost kindliness. (*See* Advertisement.)

23. Why this insulting reference to my own endlessly patient and at all times helpful publishers Futura? Could it be pique that they used a photograph of the *Sun*'s second loveliest page 3 girl, Gillian Duxbury, on the cover of *Both the Ladies and the Gentlemen* in spite of frequent and rather embarrassing representations from Emma Jane that they should use one of her?

24. I have been able to discover that Mr Wrack did not write this letter to Emma Jane. In fact, these entirely sensible

remarks appeared in Mr Wrack's thoughtful *News of the World* column and were sent to Emma Jane for comment by a lady in Derby. I suppose Emma Jane thought it would be more amusing to make facetious sport with Mr Wrack than to offer assistance to the lady in Derby.

25. Professor Mills indeed holds the chair of medicine at Cambridge and he did write such a letter. (*The Times*, Aug 21st 1976.) Needless to say, Emma Jane has never met him, and I have to say I find this constant claiming of acquaintanceship with distinguished people rather tiresome.

26. More trickery. Miss Proops's letter seems rather guarded, so perhaps this seasoned old warhorse smelt a rat.

27. This must be a joke. If Dopey Linda is in as bad a way as Emma Jane suggests, how could she write scripts for Lord Hailsham? In fact she writes articles for *The Times* under the name Ronald Butt.

28. This reference to my son Charles, who for ten years hasn't given me the slightest cause for concern (indeed I haven't even seen him), strikes me as being in very poor taste. If my boy sleeps in his jewellery, my boy sleeps in his jewellery and that's all there is to that.

29. No, it was Norman Mailer describing George Foreman the American heavyweight in training for his fight against Cassius Clay.

30. *The Guardian*, August 2nd 1976.

31. *Proceedings of the Aristotelian Society*, 97th Session, Paper 5.

32. "Latin America. An Army captain, Pedro, has twenty Indians tied up against a wall. He is about to shoot them when Jim, an English botanist, happens along. Pedro offers Jim a choice: 'You shoot one of them or I shoot them all.' What should Jim do?" *Utilitarianism, For and Against*, J.J.C. Smart and Bernard Williams (Cambridge University Press, 1973). Professor Williams uses this example as a reminder that we are not all single-minded utilitarians, for the question of what Jim should do *does* give us pause, whereas for a utilitarian the answer is easy and obvious. Dr Paskins, in fact, was interested in his paper in raising a more specific question than perhaps Emma Jane realised: namely, what are the sources of our non-consequentialist scruple over (to use a question-begging phrase) giving in to Pedro?

33. Here, it seems to me, Emma Jane picks the wrong

target and then proceeds to miss it by a mile. An enthusiastic, if somewhat scatter-brained Wittgensteinian, she follows the master in holding that human actions, human decisions, human intentions, the whole area of man's life as an agent, in fact — his activities, and the decisions that lead up to his activities — aren't capable of being causally explained. She therefore believes that there can be no such thing as a science of human behaviour, that there can be no such thing, that is to say, as psychology and sociology as these are usually conceived by their professional practitioners, let alone by enthusiastic lady amateurs in North London. Fair enough. But Ms Raeburn, as far as I know, has never claimed, on the basis of having read and misunderstood half a Penguin, to be an expert on anything under the sun. So why does Emma Jane pick on her? There is some animus here, and if Emma Jane cannot be persuaded not to write another book, the story behind this strange outburst will no doubt emerge.

34. *Letters to Russell, Keynes and Moore*, Ludwig Wittgenstein (Basil Blackwell, 1974). "Sagt der 'Satz vom zureichenden Grunde' nicht einfach, das Raum und Zeit relativ sind? Dies schneint mir jetzt ganz klar zu sein; denn alle die Ereignisse von denen dieser Satz behaupten soll, dass sie nicht eintreten können, könnten überhaupt nur in einer absoluten Zeit und einem absoluten Raum eintreten. (Dies wäre freilich noch kein unbedingter Grund zu meiner Behauptung.) Aber denke an den Fall des Massenteilchens, das, allein in der Welt existierend, und seit aller Ewigkeit in Ruhe, plötzlich im Zeitpunkt A anfängt sich zu bewegen; und denke an ähnliche Fälle, so wirst Du — glaube ich sehen — das KEINE Einsicht a priori uns solche Ereignisse als unmöglich erscheinen lässt, ausser *eben in dem Fall* das Raum und Zeit relativ sind."

35. As far as I know Emma Jane has never met Auberon Waugh. I think the explanation of this peculiar passage must be that this is a state of affairs she'd very much like to rectify. Certainly she is a great admirer of his work. It seems to me, therefore, that she is indulging in a kind of verbal *frotteurisme*, rather in the way that randy theatre critics sometimes insult young actresses whom in truth they fancy.

36. This is certainly a misprint. Emma Jane is referring to Mr Ian Sproat M.P., the courageous scourge of the social security scroungers.

37. Manifest nonsense. These two gracious artistes, who for

centuries have adorned the British stage with tact and distinction, have never been guests in our drawing-room. Were they to favour us with a visit, however, I'm confident they would behave with all the propriety they displayed in Mountain Ash, Glamorgan.

38. Once again Emma Jane, in her excitement at having an eminent sexologist within her sights, completely misses the target. I went to the trouble of looking up Ms Mooney's article in *The Daily Express* about open marriage and it struck me as perfectly sensible. Emma Jane's demonstration of the well-known fact that from a contradiction anything at all can be inferred is free of mistakes, but since "open marriage" is not a contradiction of the sort she wants, her whole letter misses the mark, if elegantly.

39. I am baffled by this letter. I find it hard to believe that Lord Goodman would write to Emma Jane. She did receive such a letter, however, so I can only conclude that it is an extremely clever forgery. Emma Jane took it to be genuine and her reply to Lord Goodman must have caused him some surprise. It is no doubt typical of him, however, that he had not only the courtesy to write back, but also the acuity to correct her error in logic.

40. Emma Jane is going to miss Sir Robert Mark. This prim old podge from Glasgow promises to provide very few laughs.